Susan Law Davenport
March 1979

TRY
MARRIAGE

BEFORE
DIVORCE

Other books by James E. Kilgore

Billy Graham the Preacher
Pastoral Care of the Hospitalized Child
Being a Man in a Woman's World
Getting More Family Out of Your Dollar
Being Up in a Down World
Letters on Life and Love

TRY
MARRIAGE

BEFORE
DIVORCE

James E. Kilgore

WORD BOOKS
PUBLISHER
WACO, TEXAS

TRY MARRIAGE BEFORE DIVORCE
Copyright © 1978
by Word, Incorporated, Waco, Texas 76703

ISBN 0–8499–0056–5
Library of Congress catalog card number: 78–57551
Printed in the United States of America

To Ruth, my partner in
the adventure of marriage

Contents

1.

The Escape Hatch:
Use It or Close It!

RECENTLY I SAT IN A church and watched a young bride and groom pledge their love. Theirs was a beautiful occasion—a handsome groom, a lovely bride, and hundreds of well-wishers gathered to witness their vows and celebrate their happiness. But would it last? In the United States nearly one in two happy young couples will be legally separating or divorcing in less than ten years.

For most the key to their dissatisfaction will be not in the failure of their sincerity but in the existence of a way to escape when things get tough. Divorce is like the hatch on a submarine. When you go underwater, you must use it to escape or close it for survival! The couple who leaves the hatch slightly ajar discovers that they drown.

I am convinced that the majority of couples cannot be emotionally committed to each other because they have yet to settle the divorce issue. Few married people have not experienced the question of what being divorced is like. Some envy single people.

"If I weren't married, I'd . . ." is the beginning sentence of the temptation. Not all such thoughts end in divorce. Many, however, as soon as they are divorced, forget what they *would* have done and begin to seek to be married again.

"If it weren't for you . . ." is a favorite marital game played by unconvinced partners. They say the unhappiness in their marital system is too great to stand, but remain married. The pain isn't quite enough to cause the system to rupture, but the rewards are discounted.

Marriage demands a commitment unparalleled in other institutions. When you join a church, you can leave its membership. When you enter school, you can fail or be graduated. When you marry, for most folks, it's for life or "until death do us part."

One couple writing their vows changed that line to read, "As long as God gives us the strength to love each other." The bride teasingly said, "If we don't make it, that way it will be God's fault, not ours!" Unfortunately, we cannot evade our responsibility that glibly.

Marriages that are like traps only breed discontent. A relationship between two spying partners breeds suspicion and distrust. Each assumes the other has his own best interest in mind and automatically has become the enemy. The *controlling* marriage is a fast-paced road to divorce. When one partner decides no longer to struggle for the control, the jig is up.

The *competitive* marriage often breeds indifference toward the other. Couples who strive together toward a goal are drawn closer. Couples who compete against each other for achievement needlessly destroy their intimacy. Competition is a distancing factor. The respect one has for an opponent is distinctively different from the desirable respect of people married to each other.

The *complementary* marriage fulfills the basic needs for companionship in two lives. Differences are accepted and respected. Neither partner demands change from the other. Both may willingly offer changes as a further strength to their complementary balance. Each partner's distinction can be appreciated as bringing variety to the relationship. Since divorce is basically a statement of irreconcilable difference, the truly complementary relationship is at the opposite pole of human experience.

Trying in marriage begins with that sense of commitment which says, "I do not *have* to live with you, but I *choose* to, happily." That declaration of intent, supported by a disciplined course of seeking mutual supportiveness, brings full joy to a couple. The escape hatch from marriage has been locked down. While it may need to be checked regularly, it will not be opened in the trials under the sea of life's pressure. Its secure fasteners represent the continuing commitment of the couple to seek marital pleasure with each other.

Often it is the subtle pleasure to please others rather than our partner that tempts us to use the escape hatch called divorce. But that's my next chapter; read on.

2.

Your Marriage—Not Theirs!

GOOD MARRIAGES CAN end in divorce. As surprising as that may sound, many bad marriages last while good ones fail.

Charles and Violet had been married thirty-two years when I first saw them. Divorce seemed imminent. They rarely communicated verbally. He felt put down and regularly pouted about it. She felt shut out and was angry at him most of the time. Their system of behavior *justified* each other's reactions. They had had little sexual contact in the last sixteen years. "You know whose fault that is," Violet said. Charles retorted, "I certainly do!" I surprised them by saying I couldn't decide.

This "bad" marriage has lasted well over thirty years, and my guess is that some newspaper will have the couple's picture in it when they celebrate their fiftieth anniversary! I call it a *bad* marriage; they experience it as an unsatisfactory relationship, but neither of them has the courage to live alone. They need each other but cannot openly acknowledge that they do. Their marriage is characterized by regular fights, occasionally physical ones, and they rarely speak to each other, even in public gatherings, such as their regular attendance at a couples' church school class.

A marriage can be nothing more than a legal contract that binds two adults to each other. These two felt bound by the legality and the morality they had been taught. But that was not the negative part of their relationship: the central destructive elements were characterized by the absence of courageous confrontation and open negotiation. Each of them invested more energy in maintaining distance than in building toward intimacy. Though legally, physically, and societally they had become partners, the emotional battle lines were clearly drawn. At the basic interactional level they were enemies. Each respected the strength of the other; neither dared risk vulnerability in the relationship.

Charles said, "It's like living with a rattlesnake. If you don't disturb it, you are safe. If it moves, you maintain your distance. All you trust is your ability to get away." He was able to escape in the newspaper, the television, or a book. Yet he rarely felt relaxed because he had to be aware of where Violet was at all times.

Violet voiced her frustration, but never put it into action. "Why does he stay with me if he won't talk or react in any way?" She felt rejected and alone. But she had enough of life's comforts to remain with him.

Theirs was a standoff: no winners but no apparent losers. After a few sessions together, I asked if either of them could offer a step toward compromise. Neither of them was willing to take this first step in negotiating a change. Counseling sessions served only as a face-saving device, so I terminated with them. They have tried three other therapists since I saw them, but the results have been the same.

Charles and Violet clearly illustrate that marriages are maintained from within. The powers of society, parents, therapy, or clergy cannot penetrate a marital system—even a destructive one—where the partners do not choose change.

Contrast that couple with Harriet and Donald, married ten years. They have two children, one of them born with a major physical impairment. Their "storybook" marriage was praised by relatives from both sides in their small city of origin. She was a beautiful bride, and he was a promising young professional man. Their marriage was characterized by a lot of verbal communication—most of it very loud! They fought battles openly and usually ended their arguments with a passionate time in bed. Their crisis in the birth of their handicapped child pulled them closer together and to their expressed faith in God. But after ten "good" years, Harriet met a man with whom she had an affair. Even though Donald tried to accept what had happened and to work to restore their relationship, it ended in divorce. Through therapy both of them adjusted fairly well. Each has since remarried and feels much better about the current relationship.

If marriages that last are good and marriages that end are bad, these couples have nothing to teach us. But both of them have a deeper than surface significance. As I have reflected on these couples, a significant insight has developed for me: Couples whose external needs are greater stay together. Couples who have overriding internal needs often divorce.

An internal need is a basic part of the personality which one has faced maturely and has learned to handle through compensation. That's healthy. An unacknowledged internal need may be the fuel for a defeating and dissatisfying pattern of behavior. Charles and Violet talked divorce and threatened each other regularly. Neither of them wanted to live alone, but each feared the the disapproval of family and friends. Donald and Harriet were driven by more compelling internal pressures and risked the disapproval of relatives and acquaintances.

In any judgment, Donald and Harriet are both stronger and healthier people than Charles and Violet. Why didn't their marriage succeed? The answers are complex, but deserve attention. Let me suggest four causes for the failures of good marriages—marriages between relatively healthy adults that appear to have the possibility of happy relationships.

Unrealistic Expectations

Both Donald and Harriet expected too much from their relationship. It failed because no union could meet the high standards they mentally set.

Both of them acknowledged that their marriage met *most* of their needs but not quite *all* of them. Donald's preoccupation with his rising career drained much of his energy. Harriet felt taken for granted, then unattractive, and finally resentful as she progressed down unhappiness lane.

One of their unrealistic expectations was that each of them could meet every need of the other. So satisfying had been their early courtship that each anticipated *total* fulfillment in their marriage. Harriet read books about being "everything your husband needs." She worked hard at her roles—femme fatale and sensuous seductress, gourmet chef and gracious hostess, relaxed mother and educator, well-read conversationalist, and social representative. She wove her own web of failure.

Donald also had high expectations of himself. Provider, achiever, family head, passionate lover, community leader, church official—he wore each title proudly and juggled the time demands somewhat successfully. The birth of his second and handicapped child, "tore me out of my frame," as he described it.

With so many major expectations for each other being fulfilled, gradually Donald and Harriet began to concentrate on what each was not getting out of the relationship. Innocently at first, Harriet shared some of her disappointments in marriage with a male friend. He seemed to understand and verbally comforted her. As they grew closer, new levels of intimacy developed. Finally a sexual relationship was begun.

When Donald discovered what had happened, he was hurt. His disappointment soon turned to indignation and then to rage.

"Even though she broke off with him, I still keep seeing that picture in my mind of the two of them making love," he said bitterly. For several months the two of them wrestled with their relationship, but finally gave up.

Marital expectation levels are raised through our experiences. When some needs are met, it becomes easier for us to expect that others may be fulfilled. The media—movies, television, magazines, books—push us in this direction. Some experiences seem routine and we wish for variety and new stimuli. When our uplifted levels of hope are not met, we are disappointed. Discontent breeds and soon infects our entire thought process. What once seemed harmless now becomes a major threat.

Unintegrated Self-Liberation

A second force that spoils good marriages is unintegrated self-liberation. The subtlety of this process is disarming! Certainly each of us wants to grow, and married persons should continue to improve themselves mentally, physically, and spiritually. But one of the most common of complaints in marriage is "we grew apart."

Given time to adjust, a good relationship can absorb almost any change. Most of us, however, tend to expect others to learn instantly what we take time to absorb. Donald was no exception. After he and Harriet were married, he continued in professional education. He also enrolled in a growth experience with a local psychologist through which he became more sensitive to his own needs. As his self-consciousness was raised, he sought as many in-depth experiences as he could have. At first he tried to talk to Harriet, but soon felt she didn't understand and talked instead to people he had met in his group. The distance at home increased.

What contributed to that distancing process between Donald and Harriet was not his self-liberation. The problem was lack of communication and integration. Donald gave up too easily in his efforts to share, and Harriet reacted to his time away rather than to his experiences.

When a spouse feels good about what is happening in his life, but experiences rejection from his marital partner, the seeds of distrust are sown. As a pattern of lack of understanding develops, other sources more likely to be receptive and positive are sought. Donald found emotionally satisfying relationships. While Harriet was recognizing her needs more slowly and chose a more specific physical way to attempt fulfillment, each of them suffered from the absence of integration of their insights into the marriage.

Liberating or growing experiences in the life of one of the partners need not threaten every marriage. Enhancement of the relationship is possible by taking the time to share and absorb those changes within the marital pattern. Some specific directions are given for this process later in the book.

Growing together, although at different rates of progress, is essential to the quality of a husband-wife union. Here are three basic tests for integration of growth. Check your relationships:

First, healthy self-growth produces change. Viewed as a system, the relationship requires time to adjust to the introduction of new data. Any change within one partner requires change in the other. Donald could not change without impacting in some way his relationship to Harriet. The test question to be applied in any marriage is: have you recognized what complementary change you are requiring of your partner as a result of your growth?

The second vital question: have you allowed sufficient time for the change in this relationship to occur? Many couples ask how long should it take. Since two people are involved, the process usually takes twice as long. For instance, a wife begins a process of liberation and after a year judges the results to be satisfactory. Her "newness" pleases her. She should allow at least one year, preferably two, before she decides her husband cannot adjust to the "new woman" she has become. In practical terms, the process is not a clean and independent one which takes place within either spouse, but instead a gradual stimulus response pattern grows within the marriage.

The third test of integration of self-growth concerns the possibility for negotiation: can the partners make the required adjustments in balance? Much like two children on a seesaw, husbands and wives rise and fall in response to each other. A willingness to push and to glide is required. Jackson and Lederer describe the process as the "quid pro quo" —a basic "give to get" procedure.

When self-liberation omits recognition of demand for modification in the spouse, is impatient with the time required, or fails to negotiate the alterations required in the relationship, distance increases. Sometimes the distance becomes too great for reconciliation.

Unchecked Assumptions

A third contributor to marital decay is an unexamined assumption. Early in their marriage Donald and Harriet assumed the best for each other. This process created openness and willingness to share with each other. Each believed the other's love and support would bring more pleasure than harm. Over the years they gradually began to assume a more negative posture. The meanings behind actions were dealt with internally but not clarified by communication. Harriet saw Donald's time away from her as "avoidance."

"He *never* enjoyed being at home or just taking *me* somewhere alone," she said, in one of our early individual sessions. "We *always* had to have someone else with us."

Parenthetically, the words *always* and *never* are excellent indicators of unchecked assumptions. When your speech is sprinkled with those words, it's time for a check-up of your unacknowledged thoughts.

Harriet suffered from her own thoughts about Donald as well as from her assumptions about others' behavior. She fantasized that other marriages were happier than her own. "I'm so envious of Cecille and Jerry; they look so happy together," she said angrily. Whether the couple she described were really happy I do not know, but in Harriet's mind they were. Her belief was not challenged by reality-testing. Her conclusion then was an unfounded "fact"—other married couples get along better than we do.

Donald also assumed for Harriet that she was "happy" with herself and did not want to change. He met other wives in his encounter group. He presumed their husbands supported their efforts toward growth and guessed that each of their marriages was better than his own. He became increasingly angry at Harriet, feeling she was limiting his own growth by her unwillingness to risk new experiences. Based on his assumption of her feelings, he began saying less about his own attitudes and interaction at home. Communication was reduced to the minimum level; Harriet sensed she was being "shut out."

Both of them contributed to the failure of their marriage in allowing these suppositions to go unchecked.

Unfavorable Comparisons

A final contributor to the failure of basically hopeful relationships occurred with this couple. Each of them longingly looked back to easier periods when they felt "in love" and unfavorably compared those times to the present circumstances.

Preoccupation with either the past or the future causes one to use the present ineffectively. The problem compounds itself when one reaches back for "the good ol' days."

Occasionally a couple can re-establish their priorities by examining the past, but Donald and Harriet expected to live at "peak" levels most of the time. Such irrational demands could cause any marriage to suffer. To seek the exhilaration of early infatuatory experiences as a constant norm for one's marriage is debilitating. This state would be not only impractical to maintain in the face of other adjustment pressures, but might also be undesirable even if it were possible. The excruciatingly exciting pleasure of orgasm is breathtaking in its stimulating thrill, but what couple could live with that peak of intensity around the clock? Similarly, the intense moments of intimacy are made more desirable by the balance of times less emotionally potent.

The human mind tends toward fickleness. In our high moments we block out the memory of low periods. In uninspired times we tend to forget days of high resolve and accomplishments. We treat our marriage with similar lack of perspective. When we feel "in love," we cannot foresee every experience that could be otherwise. Or, at moments of discouraging despair, we are predisposed toward accepting permanent defeat.

A final glimpse at Donald and Harriet will illustrate this. Prior to the birth of their second child, each felt their marriage had been "made in heaven." When through crisis experience they were disillusioned with each other, they felt doubly disappointed in comparing their feelings to earlier ones. Had they come to counseling before additional wedges came into their relationship, perhaps the conclusion would have been different. An awareness of how those unfavorable comparisons contributed to the demise of an otherwise good marriage could possibly have saved it.

Charles and Violet, by contrast, do not now suffer from unrealistic expectations. Each expects little from the other, and most of that is negative. Both essentially lead defensive lives in relation to each other. Each has assumptions borne out by antagonistic behavior from the spouse. Neither appears to be striving for self-liberation.

If your marriage sounds like either of these, it is time to stand inspection. Divorce is often the end of what could have been a good marriage. Toleration is not the ground of a satisfying relationship. At least 50 percent of marriages are not as satisfying as the partners would desire. Something happens to men and women who marry—and it isn't always good.

Good marriages develop through correct and consistent efforts at building balance and intimacy. Unsatisfactory relationships result from unexamined patterns of imbalance and ineffective communication of feelings.

Trying—not tolerating—is the beginning step toward improving marriage.

3.

I'm Still a Woman

"I'M STILL A WOMAN," Elaine sobbed in angry frustration, "but Steve treats me like a piece of furniture."

And she was every inch a woman—pretty, a willowy figure, attractively dressed. In fact, she would have drawn a second look from any red-blooded man. Yet, ignored and rejected by her husband, she had in desperation come to me for help.

Steve and Elaine, both thirty-five, were married thirteen years ago shortly after college graduation. Their children, carefully planned, were eight and five, both healthy and apparently well adjusted. Steve was a successful businessman, a community leader, and an attentive father. What Elaine found missing in her life was romance. She had read the books about being sexy when he came home, but everything she tried seemed to fail.

"Other men notice me, but I want Steve's attention. What can I do?"

Steve probably didn't realize how fortunate he was. Elaine

had not turned her frustration into that almost unquench-
able desire for response from any man. Seeing her and feeling her pain as she talked, I thought of numbers of women
I had met who had turned to other men for the satisfaction
they wanted at home. Elaine was ripe for such an involvement, but, to her credit, she sought professional help rather
than slipping into an affair.

As I counseled with Elaine, it became apparent that her
problem was not one of attractiveness but of insecurity. Steve
had discovered early in their marriage that Elaine needed
approval and affection and that by withholding these things
he gained great power in the relationship.

Elaine was not alone in her feelings. Many women feel
uncertain about their attractiveness, but the code words
differ. For Elaine it was inattention; for others it is being
taken for granted, in the sense of being a paid housekeeper
or a robot who receives no personal respect and affection.

Still other women feel unattractive because of events.
They complain of being unable to regain the good looks
they had B.B.C. (Before Baby Came), no matter how they
may diet and exercise.

Fortunately, a woman who feels uncertain about her attractiveness can do something with her problem. The key
question is how. Let me suggest three guidelines: faith,
attention, and response.

Believe in Yourself

The attractive wife believes in herself as she is—spirit and
body. She is secure in her relationship with her husband,
and she has faith in God. Her self-confidence generates a full
curiosity and a willingness to risk sharing with others. She
can encounter her world openly rather than covertly. She
doesn't need games and gimmicks for her relationship with
her husband. Her willingness to explore and to learn, to

listen to her thoughts and feelings and to know herself
creates an exciting inner world. Firm in her faith, she can
safely risk sharing those feelings with her husband. Your
belief in yourself and your attempts to share what you are
with your husband—that's an important key to inner attractiveness.

Be Attentive

A second key is attentiveness—the quality of listening per-
ceptively and responding accurately. One of the great
attributes of pleasing conversationalists is the ability to
listen. Listening to others makes them feel important. A
woman who has learned to be attentive never lacks a sense
of personal response; people around her, her husband included, gladly give her positive returns on her investment
in them.

From that assured position she shares her resources, but
does not dominate conversations. She can be comfortable
without being the constant focus of attention herself. The
self-conscious woman, on the other hand, is unable to focus
attention on another for fear of "losing" something herself.
Her uncertainty calls for continual reassurance from her
husband—or perhaps other men.

Self-conscious people—women or men—are rarely attractive. Their pride leaves them only time for personal concern.
They are absorbed in the impressions they make on others
and dominated by their need to win approval. Since the
good feeling of another's satisfaction is a fleeting experience,
insecurity robs self-conscious people of lasting positive regard for themselves.

The woman who feels dissatisfied with the feedback she
gets from her husband may have lost focus. When she no
longer clearly sees her own resources or concentrates on what
she can share, she begins to focus instead on her deficiencies

—or her husband's. Feeling self-pity, she misdirects her attention. The more self-centered she becomes, the more completely she destroys her attractiveness.

Be Responsive

Responsiveness is the third characteristic of the attractive woman. She spontaneously gives of herself—the special ingredient that no one else possesses. "I love you" is the expression of a heart full of care, concern, and a certain commitment. Those words may initiate a response and often symbolize the feeling of responsiveness. Love is the only adequate response to love. When a man or woman fails to receive what he feels is an appropriate reaction to his expression of love, doubt results. Subtle changes occur.

Changing Perceptions

Rarely does a man or woman "fall out of love." Few people who felt physically attracted to each other realize that they have experienced changes in their perceptions. Instead, when their expectations fail to be met, they read negative emotional reactions around their perceptions. This changes their feelings of love. Let me illustrate.

Bill met Barbara in college. He "fell head over heels in love" with her, and they were married within a year. When I saw them, I asked what attracted them to each other. Bill said punitively, "I've asked myself that many times!" Barbara was hurt by his comments, but it didn't sting as much as the first time she heard it. I asked if Barbara had changed; Bill didn't know.

What I saw was a man 5'6" tall, weighing approximately 150 pounds. He had a mustache and looked older than his twenty-eight years. She was a rather stocky 5'9", probably weighing 145. He was of medium frame and she seemed large-boned. She was attractive in her own unique way, but a good deal of that special feeling Bill initially experienced seemed to have been lost.

As I explored further, I discovered that Bill's mother was also a stocky woman of about the same build as Barbara. Also, like his mother, Barbara was bright, articulate, and efficient. There the similarity ended. Barbara was not sympathetic, Bill said, as his mother had always been. One can see that Bill expected Barbara to function in his mother's role—to support him in his discouraging times as she had done. When he began to feel disappointment at Barbara's lack of support during the early years of marriage, he retaliated by stopping his praise of her. As he withheld affection and didn't tell her she turned him on sexually, their sexual activity decreased.

Barbara assumed she had done something wrong and pleaded with him to tell her how she had failed. Bill couldn't verbalize his feelings clearly. He resorted to the typical, "I guess I just don't love you anymore" or "I just don't feel turned on like I once did." In fact, Barbara was doing nothing differently. Bill's perceptions of her physical attractiveness had been altered by an inner emotional process he had not fully shared with her. His expectations had not been met; he took his disappointment out on her.

When they began to communicate those hidden feelings, two changes occurred.

Bill felt relieved of the hostile burden he had within himself. Barbara began to understand his struggle and experienced a new release of energy to respond to his needs. His reaction was to become interested sexually. Result: Barbara felt attractive again, and they had some new mutual goals toward which to work.

This kind of positive change results from learning to communicate and negotiate differences which divide us. Beyond aging or weight, few changes occur in married people.

The differences lie in our perceptions. We feel positive about changes we choose and negative about those in which we identify change through manipulation.

Husbands or wives, if you identify in your behavior with Elaine or Barbara, examine your own faith, attention, and response patterns. Don't assume failure; start where you can to bring change to your marriage today.

4.

Being a Husband

CAN YOU IMAGINE a want ad for a husband? It might read like this: "Wanted—maturing young male for position as husband and probably father. No experience needed. On-the-job training. Low salary but possible high fringe-benefit package."

Being a husband—plus the usual added role of father—is the most frequently acquired position for which the applicant has little or no training. One factor is that so many men view being a husband and/or father as an adjunctive role. A part of this male stance is the result of our conditioning. Men are trained to make a living first and to share relationships secondarily. The opposite is basically true for women.

Ask a little boy what he wants to do when he grows up, and he'll respond nine out of ten times with a vocational responsibility such as "doctor," "engineer," "minister," or "politician." When a little girl is queried, she'll most often respond with "Be a mommy or get married."

For some years I have used a husband-wife exercise which

begins with the question, "Who are you?" My records of their responses show that 79 percent of the husbands gave functional or responsibility answers—professional designations, vocational titles, or types of occupations. Eighty-four of one hundred wives responded with a relationship designation such as wife, mother, or daughter.

Past Examples and Present Responses

Few men experience homemaking as a full-time vocation. Most "husband" and "father" definitions come from past examples and present responses. Too often past and present feedback is unsatisfactory.

Mel was an angry young man when I met him. He was in my office because his wife had pressured him to seek counseling. "When do I have time in my life to do what I want?" he asked, rhetorically. He looked surprised when I said, "Now." His story sounded like others.

He married right out of college and went to work for a public accounting firm. He worked hard and was promoted quickly. Transfers to new jobs, community involvement, and children took their share of his energies. Rebecca had her own plans for her husband. Mel, who avoided conflict in most relationships, chose to acquiesce rather than struggle. A pattern soon developed in which Rebecca was free to do most of the things she wanted. Soon she developed a sense of possessiveness toward Mel. When he wasn't at work, she wanted him to do things with her. She considered his time off "her time."

Many married women view men—husbands and sons—as personal possessions. Rebecca was following the example she saw in her mother. When she said "Mel is my husband!" I had no doubt that the emphasis was on the possessive pronoun.

Mel contributed to their problem by being passive. Re-

becca complained louder and demanded more. He retreated
further and avoided much interaction with her. This resulted in sexual impotence. His family physician referred
them to me. Mel had demonstrated the ultimate marital
retreat, sexual withdrawal.

After weeks of indirect attacks on each other, Mel finally
talked about Rebecca's possessiveness. As he expressed his
anger directly, Rebecca gained more security in their interaction and began to release some of the emotional hooks
she used to keep Mel close.

Nothing can be deadlier for a man's sense of personhood
than to feel possessed. In his heart he realizes the condition
is the result of his own weakness. He is angry at his wife, but
the greater wrath is toward his failure to be honest and
straightforward with his own feelings.

Some husbands assert themselves with other women, but
that usually only adds guilt to their inner emotional struggle. Some express their feelings by sexual withdrawal as
Mel did. Still others become obsessed with a new interest.

Most wives experience this indirect expression of anger
as neglect. She feels "taken for granted" or interestingly
enough, "treated like a possession—a piece of furniture!"
Remember Elaine's complaint in the last chapter? Sounds
familiar.

When Husbands Neglect Their Wives

The greatest emotional crime a man commits is to take
his wife for granted. Yet that is the most common of complaints among wives. When a man deliberately ignores his
wife, it is likely to reflect a power struggle between them.
When there is no apparent conflict, I have discovered three
contributors to a husband's neglect: preoccupation, promotion, or presumption.

Preoccupation

To be exciting to his wife, a man must experience personal stimulation regularly. But when he is preoccupied with his own needs, he is likely to miss the cues from his personal and professional environment. A self-centered and self-defeating cycle desensitizes him to the needs of others. Constantly aware of his own needs, he feels empty but somehow cannot receive. Only when he risks some vulnerability toward others can he gain that exciting response he seeks. When his focus is limited and controlled, possibilities for change slip by daily. The results tend to be debilitating. He knows he is in a downward spiral toward a crash but keeps his hand on the throttle stick. At the extreme, unchecked negative preoccupation can lead to psychosis. At best it produces a neurotic and unattractive personality.

Tom had a preoccupation problem. He was forty-three and experiencing what is commonly referred to as "male menopause." Simply put, he engaged in negative and neurotic emotional navel-watching. He attempted in every way he could identify to hide his inadequacies. The physical changes showed up first.

Tom bought a new wardrobe and a new sports car. He joined the health club to lose weight and to get in better shape. He wanted more attention from his wife, Jane, but didn't know how to ask for it. When what he did for her positive response resulted in criticism, he substituted the compliments and thoughtfulness of his younger secretaries. From them Tom got what he wanted—positive emotional stroking. He enjoyed lunch out a few times a month with younger women, and they got time off without hassles.

Like most extramarital encounters, these "harmless lunches" were justified in Tom's thinking as good for office morale, merely a public relations function of his job. Jane began to object to these activities. Tom exploded and retaliated with charges about her insensitivity to his needs. He accused her of growing old, fat, and lazy. That triggered a real fight which brought them to counseling.

Both Jane and Tom soon began to sense an emotional history to the physical and activity changes he had been experiencing. Long before buying the new clothes and car Tom had felt an inner decay. As he focused more on his internal emptiness, a sense of defeat began to grip him. He had longed for Jane to help him overcome this feeling, but she was involved with the children and their activities and had seemed not to sense his struggle. He had sunk more deeply into his depression, and the attempts to cover his private conflict resulted only in surface changes.

Instead of courageously reaching out to Jane, Tom turned to resources outside the marriage. Jane legitimately if lamely pleaded her responsibilities in the home. When they finally had an honest confrontation, they almost fell into each other's arms in my office. A strange but predictable phenomenon occurred. Tom's extremely demanding job which had required twelve to fourteen hour days suddenly seemed less pressuring. In fact, he was coming home early to have a few quiet moments with Jane before dinner. Jane too changed. She even left the children with a sitter and went on a weekend business trip with Tom.

The strange phenomenon? The same emptiness Tom dared not expose to Jane became the space she felt she could fill in his life. The distance between them that she had avoided facing disappeared when she reached out to touch Tom in his pain. The darkness of emotional preoccupation is dispelled by a loving light.

Promotion

Look at another scene.
John neglected his wife and suffered damage in the mar-

riage relationship as soon as they relocated in Atlanta. His company had promised that if he did well in two or three years, the next promotion would be to the home office. But Fran was unhappy with the prospect of living in a big metropolitan area and never adjusted. John leased an adequate house, but not one that Fran liked. When she complained, his response was "Let's make the best of it. It will only be a short period."

As John's "success" increased, Fran's displeasure did also. He promised her things would be better in their next move; she wanted to "live" now. The day John's promotion came through Fran filed for a divorce. That got John's attention, and they came to see me. While John accurately described Fran's behavior as nonsupportive, she responded by accusing him of neglect. As each of them pulled away from each other, the marriage was being strangled by the rope of their countercharges. When each partner focuses only on his rights, there is little left to sustain a relationship. Theirs died.

Presumption

Bill's neglect of his wife was built on a false assumption. When she wanted to return to college, he appeared supportive. So as soon as their third child entered first grade, Sue enrolled at the state university nearby. But among other miscommunications, Bill had in reality read this behavior as her desire to be totally independent. Inwardly he began to prepare himself for Sue's graduation, fearing that her new accomplishment would also give her enough freedom to seek a divorce. As a result of his fear, he gave less verbal praise to Sue, even though she managed the home, kept the children on schedule, and made the Dean's List. Sue felt shut out of his life, particularly when she made attempts to reach out and was rebuffed. When I saw Bill, he was very discouraged. As he convinced himself he was right about Sue's intentions, "evidence" mounted, and he assumed the worst. Her professors' praise, which she relished, he interpreted as seduction. Paranoid tendencies surrounded his thinking and his views of her actions.

When they finally came for counseling, their marriage was suspended by a thread. It took several sessions before Bill began to question his presumption, but eventually he and Sue were able to restore their mutual trust.

Men who take their wives for granted usually first neglect their own growth. Every man needs a balance of input for personal stimulation. Let me suggest four essential ingredients to build into your individual enrichment: physical exercise, intellectual stimulation, emotional sharing, and spiritual sensitizing. Explore them with me.

Physical Exercise

First, the physical needs we have increase with the aging process. Most of us need scheduled exercise in order to include it in our busy lives. Physician friends have insisted that a program of work-exercise is important but that recreational physical time should be included. This is most essential for the man whose job involves sitting at a desk. Athletic games, swimming, bowling, bicycling are some positive physical activities. Beyond the energy expended, the mentally absorbing aspects are also beneficial.

Some husbands and wives can combine their recreational interests with the pleasure of doing things together. Open athletic competition can serve some healthy needs in the marital relationship so long as the physical risks are carefully considered. Whatever activities are chosen, decide whether they are to be mostly recreation or mostly time together.

Mental Stimulation

Just as recreational activity is more beneficial to the body, non-work-related mental stimulation is positive for the mind. In this function, reading for pleasure is far more effective intellectual input than is reading business-related papers, journals, and books. A university course related to one's professional interests is helpful, but an avocational pursuit may have more energizing effects on the mind.

Some family activities provide both stimulation and relaxation. I recall a most refreshing Christmas week our family spent away from home. Playing Scrabble and assembling puzzles proved to be very relaxing activities. Variety is in itself an intellectual stimulant.

Emotional Sharing

Men in good physical condition with alert minds may not share on a feeling level with anyone. Intimacy is often equated with secrecy with the possible exception of sexual contact. While sexual intimacy is a vital part of a growing man's life, another non-physical level of closeness cries for fulfillment in all men.

A satisfying emotional life demands appropriate contacts with a number of men and women. Some will be more intimate than others. Each contact makes an imprint on the emotional tapestry of a man's spirit. How bland would be a weaving limited to one color! It is desirable for a man's intercourse needs to be met only by his wife, but to expect her to meet all other emotional, mental, and spiritual needs is an unrealistic burden on the marriage. Mature men and women find their own exchanges enhanced by the variety of encounters they share with others. Each partner develops a deeper emotional soil from which to reap a harvest to share with his own spouse.

Spiritual Sensitivity

The capstone of the inwardly rich male is spiritual sensitivity. Emotional intimacy and spiritual sensitivity differ in quality and content. When a man shares his spirit-soul with another, he is tapping his deepest emotional intimacy. Through prayer or opening himself to God, a man may experience a depth of relationship beyond that which he shares with a friend who is physically present. When two people exchange views or relate episodes honestly with each other and the content is God-centered, that may also be a spiritual experience.

I have discovered few men who acknowledge sharing a desirable level of emotional intimacy or spiritual exchange with their own wives. It is not unusual then to find many married men vulnerable to a relationship that begins at this level. Far too many women have experienced the feelings expressed recently by a wife: "I have his body and his money, but someone else may have his heart and soul!"

A good friend shared his personal struggle in this story. His marriage is in its twenty-sixth year, and Dick seems to love his wife deeply. They touch in public and appear to have a close relationship. As a minister, he himself does a good deal of effective marriage counseling.

"Marge and I had allowed our sexual relationship to fulfill most of our needs for intimate exchange. We didn't fight but we rarely talked at a deeper level. When the denomination asked me to accept a female associate, Marge and I talked it over. We agreed intellectually that such a working relationship would not threaten us maritally.

"I had no idea the impact that this young female minister would have on my life. She was eager to learn. Probing and stimulating questions about our ministry made the numerous hours we spent together both productively positive in our working relationship and rewarding in the closeness we developed toward each other."

"I tried to talk about Susan to Marge, but I felt helplessly vulnerable. I craved the excitement of working with Susan, but I feared the possibility of sexual involvement."

As Dick related more of his story, I learned how he had walked this emotional tightrope for four years, struggling with fatherly protection and masculine virility in his relationship to his young associate.

A man less mature than Dick might have simply settled for a sexual involvement as a resolution to one aspect of the conflict. In his own mind Dick had decided that would be wrong for him. "Marge made the difference," he continued. "When I felt ready to ask for the associate's transfer, I told her more specifically about my struggles. Her reassurance and strength was a bulwark. Susan and Bob, her husband, met with us; perhaps my openness served as a breakthrough. I feared that everything I had preached about human growth and emotional openness might not work. But what we have learned from this experience has freed us to go to new depths in our marriage, in our deeply satisfying friendship with Bob and Susan, and in our vulnerable but renewed search for more total encounters with people."

When Dick ended his story, I felt my own heart in my throat. In a significant hour I had shared in his moving awareness of who he was as a man, a husband, and a minister. His integrity and his vulnerability remained; perhaps when those two things meet, a wife can readily discover her husband.

5.

Power Struggle:
The Battles of the Sexes

IN THE MUSICAL *Oklahoma* there is a lyric that says "Anything you can do, I can do better." That is a consistent theme song in the troubled marriage. Destructive competition is present in most marriages that fail. The marital power struggle is a complicated phenomenon, but let's look at some of the parts in an attempt to clarify the issues.

Few couples marry with developed power struggles. The exceptions "fight all the way to the altar." Weddings, however, sometimes contribute to beginning discord. In an informal survey of couples coming for marital counseling, I have discovered that one in four have some complaints that reach back to the wedding plans. Disagreements over who was to be invited, how many from each family did what, and similar problems show up on the list of gripes. In exploring these conflicts further, one factor has remained consistent. The "fight style" or method of struggle exhibited as early as the wedding rehearsal remains in the marriage; that is, an aggressive bridegroom is more likely to be an aggressive husband while a passive man is likely to struggle passively in the marriage.

Sounds obvious enough, doesn't it? Yet many husbands and wives cry foul at this very point.

Take Hilda and Russ. Hilda complained that Russ would not fight with her, that to avoid a confrontation he would listen and walk around or away. When I asked about premarital patterns, Russ said he had always been taught to "hold his peace and not get mad." He was reared in a quiet family and his father had often acted the way Russ saw himself behaving. He was following his father's model.

On the other hand, Hilda was the daughter of a volatile but tenderhearted man who often shouted and accused his wife and children unfairly. Later he would apologize. In spite of his unpredictable qualities, Hilda said she felt very close to her father. Russ was, in fact, more like her mother.

As we worked together, Russ and Hilda began to see that each of them had recreated their parental patterns for handling conflict. Change was difficult, but gradually they reshaped their ways of coping with conflict. Russ and Hilda were good candidates for learning the art of negotiation. This process aids the progression of positive change and conflict resolution.

The Necessity for Conflict

There are three basic principles to the system. First, conflict is a given. The presence of conflict is a sign of emotional health. It is not only unhealthy but impossible to eradicate conflict completely. Creativity often results in the resolution of tensions. In fact, the chemistry of the body illustrates that health is the process of handling conflict. The body absorbs resources and converts them into appropriate energy cells. The marital system must also take a variety of input and transform it into the energy of mental health.

Conflict Management

The choice Russ and Hilda had was *how* to manage their conflict. That's the second principle: partners *choose* the style of conflict management. Until they faced their pattern, Russ and Hilda made no choices. Now they have tried to focus on their conflicts and work them out systematically. These six sentences helped them in their conflict management:

1. Handle it as soon as possible.
2. Don't overlook common courtesy when you confront each other.
3. Stick to the issue.
4. Listen as much as you talk.
5. Negotiate naturally. Seek compromise.
6. Anticipate reconciliation. Work toward it.[1]

By following these guidelines they avoided using the models established by his father or hers.

The Importance of Conflict Resolution

The third principle is that both partners fail if a resolution is not achieved. Russ had blamed Hilda for causing arguments, and Hilda accused Russ of frustrating her. As we examined their behavior together, they began to see that neither of them was happy. Then they could see that each of them lost in unresolved conflicts.

A second couple found the same principle helpful.

Connie and Ralph weren't speaking to each other. My

---

[1] James E. Kilgore, *Getting More Family Out of Your Dollar* (Irvine, Calif.: Harvest House, 1976) .

secretary had given me a nonverbal warning when I met them in the reception area. They began our hour by attempting to fight through me. After a few minutes I set aside my usual intake procedure, and agreed to try to help them resolve this fight so that we could proceed.

"How did the fight start?" I asked, but got little response. "Let's try *when* instead."

"It began Tuesday," Ralph finally said. "She didn't get home until after midnight."

Connie broke in here, "My flight didn't land until 10:45 P.M. By the time I wrote my report and got my luggage, it was already 11:40 P.M. It does take half an hour to drive home from the airport."

"Can you tell Connie what has upset you?" I asked Ralph. After a few hesitant attempts, he said he had wanted to have intercourse, but had fallen asleep. She had failed to awaken him when she came home. He was angry when he awoke, but left for work without waking her. It was now Friday, and neither had spoken much for three days.

Each had assumed something about the conflict. Both were too proud to ask for an explanation. When they had tried to talk, he generalized about *never* being able to depend upon her. Both of them had begun to talk but not listen. The fight had escalated.

They had lost three days of productivity in their marriage because of an ineffective power struggle. Those power struggles fall into three general designations.

Choose Your Weapons

In the "good old days" the two basic weapons were money and sex. The husband usually controlled the finances. If the wife was "a good girl," she got some money. If not, she didn't. She usually controlled the sex. If he was a "good boy," he got some; if not, he waited.

Struggles for control usually involve each partner's seeking the most advantageous "weapon" to use in response to his mate's most vulnerable point. Since money is a power symbol in most of the world, its uses as a marital weapon are fairly obvious. The apparent power of money is seductive. The promise of a gift or an inheritance is a classic example of using money to influence. Some parents attempt to manipulate adult children within this context; a mate may also seek control in the marriage relationship through this vehicle. The message is "Be nice to me or I'll leave you out of my will." In marriage conflicts I often hear a spouse say, "It is *my* money; I'll spend it any way I like!"

A more direct monetary approach is seen in the "bartering" game. "I will buy you this if—" is one of the cue sentences. A conditioned framework is established in which a prize or reward comes as a result of certain behavior. Often the exchange in the barter system can be sexual activity. A recent best-selling book for women even suggested that sexual activity could result in a new appliance.

Unfortunately, certain marital power struggles widen to include children, and even other relatives or friends. "Sides" are chosen and battle lines are drawn. Manipulations are subtle in these conflicts. Rarely are they staged openly in the presence of the spouse and those from whom support is sought. A raised eyebrow or a sustained stare may be non-verbal indications of the conflict. Secret pacts are intimated and confidences are assured when husbands or wives attempt to gain some form of emotional advantage. Divorced parents are the most obvious examples of the marital power struggle. Their attempts to gain advantages did not begin with divorce. Divorce simply makes them obvious.

Money, sex, and people are the most obvious tools in marital struggles. Religion, job security, social prestige, and other forms of emotional blackmail are also used in the arsenal of wedlock. Perhaps these struggles do reduce marriage to what one wit described as "holy deadlock."

One-Upmanship

A very subtle power struggle is the competitive, and sometimes less destructive, game of one upmanship. "Putdowns" in this game can be extremely painful, of course, like having a wound inflicted with a blade. But, in general, a more prevalent pattern is not so malicious. Instead husbands and wives subtly race against each other.

John and Jane were two young professionals. He was a lawyer and she was a physician. Their parents had supported both of them through the graduate education programs. John began his practice two years earlier than Jane, but her skills soon began to reward her financially. They kept separate accounts professionally and personally. What appeared to be a healthy his-and-hers game soon became a full-blown, and at times foolish, conflict. When he bought new office furniture, she refurbished her suite. If she purchased a new car, he immediately bought a fancier one. Their home was full of gadgets which they purchased as "surprises" for each other. Each was generous in his own way. When I finally met them, they described their relationship as competitive but not vital. One-upmanship had sapped the joy away.

Argumentative patterns are also a form of one-up/one-down conflict. Like elephants, these marriage partners never forget, especially when the other one is "wrong." Corrections may seem to be born of concern, but the spouses understand the dynamics. People around them feel uneasy, but don't always know why.

In a recent social gathering a wife interrupted her husband with "I'm sorry you're wrong, dear, but—" What followed was a not so subtle put-down both of his intelligence and his memory. Several couples were present, but no one acknowledged the one-upmanship game. Instead the subject was changed abruptly and the conversation developed along other lines.

Going for the Jugular

Perhaps the most vicious power struggles are those in which the couple not only "fights" at home in private, but in front of other people.

George and Marie invited several couples for a New Year's Eve party. Early in the evening when they made reference to each other as "the old man" or "the old lady," their friends laughed. It seemed like a cute social way to tease each other. As the evening wore on and the drinking took effect, the guests became more uncomfortable. George openly derided Marie for gaining weight. He embraced a female guest and made loud comments about how much better her body was than Marie's.

Marie was not to be outdone. At first she resolved to "win" over George by acting the part of "the gracious lady." However, before the evening was over, she was chiding George for being a "lover boy" in public but being a "let-down" in the bedroom.

I am told that all the guests left before midnight. George and Marie each blamed the other's "uncalled-for" remarks as the cause of the early departure.

When it becomes more important to make a point with your spouse than to show regard for the feelings of others, the power struggle in your marriage has reached extreme levels. Fortunately, win-lose patterns can be turned into win-win styles.

Ted was a young and somewhat insecure salesman when I first met him. Gloria, his wife, had invited me to speak at a "sweetheart banquet" for their church couples class. As we drove in from the airport, I sensed they were not getting along well in the marriage. During the evening I observed their subtle patterns of one-upmanship. Ted's "gift of gab" turned slightly cooler when directed at Gloria.

Some years later, they drove to Atlanta for consultation with me. During the time since our first meeting Ted had become openly punitive of Gloria in public gatherings. She admitted "getting back at him" by developing a relationship with his boss, which finally ended in a sexual liaison while Ted was on the road.

Their only motivation for counseling seemed to be their four children. All I could do immediately was to deal with their crisis. After spending several hours with them in one week, I referred them to a colleague nearer home who helped them develop a more permanent win-win pattern.

In win-lose situations husbands and wives fall back on their preservation instincts. In learning to move to win-win styles, each must believe that respect for the other is essential to his own emotional well-being. Ted had great difficulty with this. When I finally pointed out that criticism of Gloria was a reflection of his own poor judgment in choosing a marriage partner, the point began to come into focus.

For Ted and Gloria, trying marriage before divorce meant learning a new way of relating to each other. Their annual Christmas card is a reminder that even some very destructive patterns can be turned around by hard work to result in rewarding relationships.

6.

Marriage Is
What You Make It!

"MARRIAGE IS POSSIBLE because it combines the maximum of temptation with the maximum of opportunity."—George Bernard Shaw.

Institutions do not fail; people do. Marriage, like any other human structure, can be only as successful as its participants wish it to be. In a sense, there are no bad marriages —only poorly developed relationships masquerading under the guise of marriage.

Good marriages are not made in heaven. Fulfilling relationships are not the result of good wishes of friends, a beautiful wife and a handsome husband, or the hopes and resources of well-intentioned parents. Good marriages are worked out in the kitchen, the living room, and the bedroom, as patterns of exchange are established. Good marriages are just plain work!

Marriage is a do-it-yourself kit—a resource package composed of the skills and talents of a man and a woman. The use of those components in building varies from couple to couple. The ability to "customize" any kit is often the key to its uniqueness and service to the purchaser. The same is true for marriage. Any marital advice followed precisely or in a wooden manner will produce only limited results. Adapting the principles to your own special needs is what really makes them work.

Three pivotal elements in a marital relationship—the ability to communicate, the ability to negotiate, and the ability to incorporate—determine the success or failure of most relationships.

The Ability to Communicate

Examine communication with me. At its basic level three parts are involved: the sender, the receiver, and the message. Sounds simple enough, doesn't it? Yet most basic marriage difficulties begin at this level. Approximately 70 percent of the couples I see in therapy identify "lack of communication" as a serious problem in their marriage.

What do they mean? I often ask these four clarifying questions:

1. Does lack of communication mean you don't talk at all?
2. Does lack of communication mean that you don't understand what is said by your partner?
3. Does lack of communication mean that you don't hear what you want to hear from your spouse?
4. Does lack of communication mean your spouse doesn't listen to you?

Most of the time, each spouse sees himself as both a good sender and as a responsive receiver of marital messages; it is the partner who is not up to par.

Two cardinal laws of communication, if followed, guarantee improvement. The first is: *I am always responsible for my own thoughts, feelings, words, and actions.* I cannot give away this "right" to another. But too often I try.

Look in on Jill and Brad in a typical marital exchange. A traveling salesman, Brad arrived home late on a Friday evening and came straight to bed. Saturday and Sunday were fun family days at the houseboat. It is now Monday morning and Brad is ready to leave for another trip. "Did you wash my tan shirt?" he asks Jill. "No, I didn't have time," she replies. "You know I *need* that for my brown suit I am taking this week!" he snaps back. Brad's anger is based on the assumption that Jill knows what he is thinking. Unfortunately, Jill doesn't and shouldn't be expected to know what is in his mind. For Brad "lack of communication" means Jill doesn't read his mind.

Let's push Brad and Jill a bit further. Jill is extremely jealous of Brad's secretary whom he calls regularly when he is on the road. Often Jill feels that the secretary has more knowledge of Brad's business and personal schedule than she does. Feeling hurt and disappointed, Jill accosts Brad in the presence of friends: "Shouldn't we ask Mary before we plan something for the next weekend?" For Jill lack of communication means she doesn't hear what she wants to hear from Brad. Brad, however, cannot be responsible for Jill's jealousy. She must make her feelings known in order for him to respond appropriately.

The communication problem now escalates to a point of little or no conversation between the two of them. Change will come about only if each of them sends clear signals and has real expectations about the partner's responses.

Mixed signals create discomfort in communication. The message is not clear, and therefore, the response called for is uncertain. A mixed signal occurs when the words spoken do not match the tone or the feeling expressed by the message.

A husband may find his wife looking less than her best.

When he says, "Don't *you* look beautiful," the wife will probably be offended. If he says it jokingly and puts his arm around her, the congruence of the message is maintained by the touch so that he communicates teasing and support rather than judgment. If he communicates disgust with his words, she can respond angrily. However, the two levels— words and feelings—have left him with an escape from responsibility. Look at this:

Husband: Don't you look beautiful!

Wife (angry) : You don't look so hot yourself.

Husband: Why jump on me—I said you looked beautiful.

Here the husband escapes responsibility behind his words, but he fails to acknowledge the feelings or tone expressed by his comments.

Suppose the wife responds to his words:

Husband: Don't you look beautiful!

Wife: Thank you, dear!

Husband: Boy, you never understand what I say to you at all.

In that example the husband ignores the content of his word message and blames the wife for not having the sensitivity to respond to his feelings. There's the trap: mixed signals must be acknowledged *only* as garbled messages.

When the receiver tries to accept the responsibility for figuring out what the sender *meant* by his message, trouble results. I refer to this attempt to know what is in a spouse's mind as "playing God." When you try to say what another person *should* or what was *meant,* the result is an invitation to an argument. To play God—to assume a position of all knowing power is to invite the process of dethronement. It regularly occurs between husbands and wives.

How can this be avoided? That's where the second law of communication is helpful. It says: *Before I respond to you, I will let you know what I received.* In the case of the mixed message, I respond to the discrepancy received. Let's exaggerate our examples to illustrate:

> Husband (with a disgusted tone) : Don't you look beautiful!
>
> Wife: Is that a compliment or an attack?

Good: The decision about the husband's communication is put back where it belongs—in his lap!

Here's an even better response:

> Wife: I like compliments, but the way you said that I'm not sure I got one.

In this case the wife says what she heard and still leaves it up to the husband to clarify his message.

The second law of communication works this way: When I tell you what I heard, you know whether or not what you intended to say was received. If it was not, you can clarify your message. When the sender and the receiver function properly, the message is the communication discussed. If the sender or the receiver clouds the content of the message with the tone of unacknowledged feelings, the likelihood of misunderstanding is increased.

Mastering these two guidelines to communication is a major step to improving marriage. The ability to exchange information, feelings, and descriptions without misunderstanding is a basic building block in the marital plan. Here again are the two principles:

1. I am always responsible for my own thoughts, feelings, words, and actions.
2. Before I respond to you, I will let you know what I heard you say.

When a couple learns to communicate, they add to that process the ability to negotiate.

The Ability to Negotiate

When we looked earlier at power struggles, I listed six principles for handling conflict. The fifth of those guidelines—to negotiate naturally, to compromise—is important in dealing with the unacknowledged need to dominate that underlies most power struggles. Couples who move beyond good data exchange—the basis of good communication— make more progress as they learn to compromise effectively. They are exercising the ability to negotiate.

The word *compromise* needs some initial attention. In the meaning often associated with the word, there is a sense of negative definition. Such terms as *mutual concession, accommodation,* or *truce* are often used as synonyms for the word compromise. For our purposes the literal definition of the word is important. The Latin word *compromittere,* from which it is derived, means "to promise mutually." This root word embodies balance, positive adjustment, and agreement, and it denotes a much more positive and desirable communication of meaning.

Marital compromise is work, but an effort that satisfies both partners mutually. Competition divides, but compromise can strengthen.

Jack and Marie's use of finances—a typical area of struggle —can illustrate this principle. When they married, each of them had an apartment with furnishings. Both had good jobs, adequate bank accounts, including savings plans, and each owned a car. "We married for love," Jack said, when they first came to visit me. They were able to merge their lives and their mutually independent financial systems continued beautifully into the marriage. Expenses were divided equally, and together they were able to make a very adequate down payment on a home. Soon they were expecting a child. When Marie resigned her job a few weeks before their son's birth, she began to have some nagging doubts about the loss of financial independence.

Having always seen himself as a rather generous person, Jack felt offended when Marie first brought up the problem of her not having money of her own to spend. As they discussed their mutual needs, a compromise emerged. They would maintain a mutual budget, and in addition to their two separate accounts, establish a third. Most of Jack's salary went into the new account from which Marie was to function as family treasurer. The balance of the money was divided equally into their existing checking accounts. Each of them was free to spend from his or her own account without reporting to the other. Their compromise resulted in a mutually satisfying and freeing financial plan that had a strong strengthening effect on their relationship.

Where couples do not seek compromise, the same situation could have brought a sense of resentment and a destructive use of power to the relationship. What Jack and Marie learned to do was to compromise on the basis of needs and skills rather than on strength and control.

Jack had power in his position as breadwinner, but he willingly relinquished control because of his need to be generous and his understanding of Marie's fear of dependence. He also respected Marie's skill in handling money and was willing to have her use that ability for both of them. Marie's respect for Jack grew because of his capacity to compromise. As they talked more about her feelings, she understood her own needs more fully. She discovered that as she disclosed herself to him, she also learned to know more about who she was. Her new ability to trust and her confidence in Jack made it possible for her to make deeper personal probes into her own past.

The ability to communicate plus the ability to negotiate with each other gave them a stronger marriage.

The Ability to Incorporate

Strong marriages fuse the energy of individual strengths into the service of the conjugal union without loss to either person. Where couples communicate well and negotiate effectively, they are able to weld their resources into a strong bond.

Have you noticed how some people seem to match each other? After years of living together, they almost look alike. Physical similarities frequently contribute to this phenomenon, but many couples who do not apparently blend physically develop a sense of sharing that embodies their togetherness. This legacy of loving can be attributed to three significant qualities: a mutual enjoyment of affectionate display, a generous appreciation of differences, and a supportive assimilation of personal values. Let me elaborate.

Affection

Expression of affection is a pivotal element in marriage. Numerous husbands and wives have shared with me in confidence their great need to be touched, stroked, or held by a spouse. Too many of them are married to a person whose affectional needs differ greatly. It is not usually necessary to attempt to pursue this need back to childhood and explain the deep craving present in the light of insufficient infant or childhood stroking. Deep within each of us is a desire for love—to love and to be accepted. One of the ways we express this feeling is through physical affection—touching, holding, caressing, or stroking. In the infant, security is learned by touch—the warmth of human response and contact.

Observation has shown that adult relationships thrive on this same affectional exchange. Marriages in which a mutual enjoyment of physical affection exists are likely to be more satisfying than those without it. The level of intimacy deepens as the comfort with physical contact increases. While sexual passion is a specific and intense expression of physical drive, the affectional exchange we are talking about here provides a generalized sensual fulfillment and a feeling of comfort rather than release of tension. The warmth and gentleness experienced in the caring touch is of a different quality than the excitement of an erotic stroke. Both are present in a fulfilling marriage. The often subtle but reassuring message of physical contact conveys to the partners a sense of belonging in relationship. Each partner experiences a feeling of well-being and the assurance of a steady affection.

Appreciation

Couples who incorporate their mutual strengths within the relationship appreciate their differences. They do not stand in awe of each other but have a sincere admiration of their respective abilities and personality traits. They enjoy each other. Each makes the other feel important without sacrificing any of his own integrity. They listen to each other in public and in private—with respect. While they often function independently of each other, they feel a special anticipation about being together. Their individual experiences often provide the basis for a stimulating conversation and a doubling of the pleasures because they are again shared. Each of them has a confidence in the other which strengthens them in a crisis. The lists of benefits can be extended, and all of them blossom from the soil of that deep admiration the two share for each other.

Assimilation

The third significant ingredient—assimilation—may be described as a blending of the values of the two individuals. This quality involves more than verbalization of intellectual agreements. A growing couple experiences a mutually satisfying demonstration of the similarity of their commitments to life.

I believe it is important to distinguish between similar views and common values. A couple may blend their lives effectively without necessarily being in agreement. Their views about politics, social issues, or even religious tenets may differ; but they hold the same values about relationships. They exhibit this common value by remaining nonjudgmental toward each other, particularly when they disagree.

Values often become the controlling factor in our lives. To share common beliefs about relationships becomes then a highly important area of exchange. What we live is what we essentially believe, no matter what we say. The couple who lives out their faith in each other by respect, consideration, and adaptation to mutual needs indeed finds happiness.

Do It Yourself

These abilities require no special insights or magic formulas. What they demand is attention to detail in personal relationships. Any husband and wife who are willing to apply energy to bring them about in their marriage system can do so. Motivation becomes the key issue.

Marriages are changed by two extremely different energizing factors: the desire to cope with pain or the appetite to achieve rewarding pleasure. People seek counseling for one or the other of these two reasons. Couples come for help because they are hurting. The opposite is also true; they seek help in achieving a better relationship than the one they now know. Whichever force stirs you, there is hope. You can do it yourself; you can have a better marriage. Trying marriage fully means learning to communicate, to negotiate, and to incorporate.

7.

Broken Dreams

ONCE UPON A TIME in a land called University, a charming young prince met a beautiful young princess. Although each of them had much wealth promised them in their respective home castles, they chose to make their own way in the world.

The young prince and princess pledged themselves to love and care for each other forever. Both of them despised the meaninglessness that they had observed in their parents' castles. They set off into the wilderness. Finding a pleasant spot, the young prince built a leaning shelter. The princess found fruit, and the prince hunted the small animals for food. Soon they enjoyed a wide knowledge of their area and began to groom trees and to make their surroundings more pleasant. Before long the princess was expecting a child.

"We must have more comfortable surroundings for our child," said the princess. The prince took the last of his savings and bought a small shop and a house in the nearby village. They moved into town and were still very happy. The prince was a hard worker and spent long hours learning the proper marketing techniques for his shop. He traveled to other villages to buy goods, entrusting his own shop to his several new employees. He became well known and eventually grew quite rich.

The princess enjoyed her new baby, but missed the quiet walks at the wilderness farm with the prince. When another child was born, she felt even more responsible for caring for her children, especially since the prince spent too little time with them.

Late one evening when the prince returned home, the princess met him in her loveliest gown. She thought it was his favorite, but he did not notice because he was so concerned with business matters. This disappointed the princess very much. Finally, the prince and princess had a loud argument. Each accused the other of failing to work at their marriage. Both felt their lives had become as meaningless as were their parents' marriages.

The next day the prince took his personal possessions, gave the princess and his children most of his goods, and set out "to seek happiness again."

Each generation expects to improve on the patterns of the past. Many do. However, there seem to be certain predictable passages through which most human institutions go. Marriage also develops along certain lines to points of critical decision. One transition in husband-wife relationships can be described as a survival-to-meaning movement.

Few couples marry without the intention of remaining together happily. The initial forces in their relationship are like survival instincts. There are numerous tasks to master and skills to develop. Problems to be solved include housing, jobs, budgeting, sharing responsibilities, and so forth. Energies are demanded for these pressing needs. A pattern of coping is established early.

Later, when the house is organized, the budget is established, and perhaps children have been born, the marital partners rest long enough to ask, "What does all this effort mean?"

For some couples, the survival period takes only a few months, but for others twenty years or more may pass. Especially where children come early, the shift in attention from the diadic union to the family may be swift. "Good" parents submerge their wishes beneath the needs of their children, usually at the expense of the marriage. Perhaps twenty years later, when the children leave home, Mom and Dad (what happened to their first names or endearing nicknames?) find they have each other again and must reexamine what their marriage now means to them.

Meaning becomes a difficult thing to assess. Philosophers debate it, but couples want to live it. Here are three areas for direction in evaluating the meaning level of a marriage: agreement, freedom, and caring.

Agreement

I saw a cute poster on an office wall recently. It showed a little boy pushing from behind a car and a little girl shoving from the front of the car in the opposite direction. They were both straining. The caption said, "Progress is when we all push together." Regrettably, a marriage is like that for many couples. They are working against each other rather than helping each other.

Understanding your mate's goals and hopes will only occur through conversation. I recently polled an audience about the amount of time the couples who were there spent talking to each other—omitting conversations where children or a third party was present. The average was about ten minutes a day. That's just a little more than one hour a week, and less than five hours a month. Time to listen is essential to understanding in a relationship, and it obviously takes more than that little amount of time.

Similarity of goals adds to a sense of meaning. Two people have difficulty achieving an end when they are moving in different directions. A theist and an atheist will conflict. Activists and philosophers often have disagreements over the appropriate methodology toward a goal. Day people and night people must make the most of their overlapping energy periods. Husbands and wives need to examine their feelings toward each other and understand themselves well enough to deal with these kinds of differences in their natures.

Agreement in the essential areas may be delineated by spelling out our priorities. Here is an exercise for clarification which I use with couples: Take a sheet of paper and make four columns on it. In the lefthand column, list your personal goals for life. Be as specific as possible. Instead of saying, "To make money," list the exact salary you would like to achieve. Don't be satisfied with "Give the kids an education"; be specific about a savings plan. But don't limit yourself to financial goals. Try to list your emotional aims as well, for instance, "To be intimate, close with each other." Or, more specifically, "To set aside time for conversation daily."

After you have completed a lefthand column, writing as many goals—or even dreams—as you can, then head the second column *priority.* The third column will be headed *progress,* and the final one should be labeled *potential.* Assign your goals to each of the columns, putting the things that must be done in order for you to maintain your present status under *priority.* Those goals which would be highly desirable but are not necessary can be placed under *progress,* and the final column, *potential,* is for the balance of your dreams.

When a husband and wife work independently at first and

then compare and combine their lists, a stimulating conversation results. Agreeing on goals in this manner makes it possible to begin to look at the action steps necessary to fulfill them. A basic agreement on the direction of the marriage is essential to shared meaning.

Freedom

One of the wall messages in my office reads, "To love someone is to give him room enough to grow." James Kennedy caught the sense of this aspect in marriage when he said: "At the heart of love there is a simple secret; the lover lets the beloved be free." Mature love is like that; immature love is possessive.

The feeling of being trapped in a relationship is a frequent cause of depression among married people. With no apparent viable options, this sense of confinement breeds meaninglessness. Meaning is the result of feeling free to contribute to the relationship and to grow within it.

People who accept each other discover meaning in their relationship. Those who attempt to remake one another will find a struggle ahead. None of us really enjoys feeling possessed.

Freedom in relationship also contributes to a feeling of independence. While dependence offers security to some people, most of us rebel against strong reminders of our needs for others. Freedom is the inner-dependent state in marriage where two recognize their willing dependence but accept the implied individual responsibility that remains with each of them.

Caring

A fine balance exists between enjoying another's freedom and expressing concern and support for that individual.

Marriage provides such a context for that delicate harmony. Caring does not require unison; it undergirds the blending of differences. This attitude in a relationship transforms the simple task into expressions of tender concern. The spirit of caring is caught in the American Indian marriage blessing:

> Now you will feel no rain, for each of you will be shelter for the other.
> Now you will feel no cold, for each of you will be warmth to the other.
> Now there is no more loneliness.
> Now you are two persons, but there is only one life before you.
> Go now to your dwelling to enter into the days of your life together.
> And may your days be good and long upon the earth.

The compassion of two who have each other's interest at heart is the caring that brings growing meaning to marriage.

The motto of the French Revolution reads: "In the essentials, unity; in the nonessentials, liberty; in the all things, charity." When married couples follow these principles, a new revolution occurs in their lives. Dreams once shattered by struggles can be restored to hope and eventually be fulfilled.

8.

What Happened When the Sun Rose?

"PARTY SUPPLIES—SICK ROOM EQUIPMENT." The marquee over the rental store caught my eye as I drove toward a speaking commitment in a California metropolitan area. I was to talk to an organization called Parents Without Partners. My mind clicked to an incident the week before in my office.

Expectations and Disappointments

Ben was a handsome, broad-shouldered, and tall graduate of a leading southeastern university. A well-known football hero, he had been married two years to Carol. Petite, blond, and curvaceous, she held a job as a model at a local department store. My first meeting with them had been rather grim. Neither of them felt much hope for their marriage. This was the second meeting, an individual session with Ben. He was not the kind to cry easily, but shortly after our visit began, tears were streaming down his cheeks. I'll probably never forget the impact of those words: "If I could only figure out what happened when the sun rose!"

He filled in the story. He and Carol came from prominent families and dated all the way through in college. She was the beauty queen, and he was the campus hero. Everybody, including the two of them, thought they would make the perfect couple.

"The party is over," Ben said bitterly, "and I feel like marriage is the hangover." Carol in a later session also expressed her disappointment at what she had experienced in their relationship.

Not all of us are football heroes or beauty queens, but after a few months or years, many of us feel like Ben and Carol did about their marriage. In the bright daylight of experience so much of the moonlight of expectation changes. Some of this results from the socialization process. From parents, older siblings, other relatives—and often, neighbors —we learn the four steps of life: "As quick as you can, grow up, marry, be a success, and retire early." The pressure to fulfill these or similar expectations begins early.

I want to focus on three common disappointments that occur between the moonlight of dating and the sunlight of marriage.

Changes in Romantic Feelings

The first is the change in the feeling of romance. Ben said, "The pursuit was fun; once I got her I sort of lost interest and she did too." Some of the implication of that statement was sexual. Carol was technically a virgin when they married. That means that they had not had intercourse, although they had petted heavily and had felt a good deal of sexual excitement.

Since they had been married they had not made much progress in their conjugal union. "I sure don't know what all the fuss was about," Carol said; "Sex is no big deal! I like being close, but I don't see rockets or hear bells. I am not sure of those who say they do."

Both Ben and Carol had been "socialized" to have great expectations for sex but instead discovered it to be a disappointing experience. A poor sexual relationship dampens romantic and intimate feelings immediately, and for Ben and Carol it was a frustrating arena. Because neither of them now expected their sexual experience to get better, they tended to avoid other physical contact and expressions of affection. The level of contact and the feelings of romance diminished quickly.

Limited Resources for Communicating and Sharing

A second disappointment for many couples is a painful awareness of their limited resources in the area of communication and shared interests. In the college world activities were planned and there were too many invitations to accept for parties and gatherings. Marriage forced Ben and Carol to talk to each other. Away from the area of sports or fashions, each of them felt woefully inadequate. Their own judgments of themselves were much harsher than others, including their judgments of each other. But that was a serious feeling to be considered. They tried tennis, but his needs were more vigorous than hers. He went shopping but felt bored; she understood. Neither of them felt they had much to offer the other.

Dating and courtship focus on social activities and romantic interest, while marriage is often more task-oriented and geared to interpersonal sharing. When the transition from a more superficial exchange to a deeper interplay occurs, the couple grows. They both begin to feel positive about themselves and their relationship.

When this passage is not successfully made, both husband

and wife feel frustration and an uneasy sense of inadequacy. "We have nothing in common any more" is a typical complaint by an anxious spouse. Each feels trapped because of his own limitations, and there is the expectation that the spouse should bring about the change. Carol described her feelings: "Ben was always the star when we were in college. He drew people and they talked to him. As a model, people look at me; they don't talk to me."

Resistance to Change

A third disappointment experienced in the sunrise of marriage is a lack of commitment to change. Every person who has married an alcoholic believing he would change has suffered this shock. As a rule people resist change. Men who did not plan dates will not suddenly become interested in social activities after a wedding band is placed on the third finger of the left hand. Women who were more concerned with how they looked than what they ate are not likely to become great dieticians in marriage. To expect the wedding vows to reform a person is unrealistic.

Marital expectations tend toward the idealistic, but marital behavior is predictably realistic. As one wit put it, "You can be married under orange blossoms, but you'll get a lemon anyway."

Lack of commitment to change is largely a matter of laziness. Few of us are willing to discipline ourselves to meet the needs of those we say we love. That process demands an energy born only of a willingness to sacrifice. Then much patience is demanded if we wait to see others sacrifice in response to us. More of us are like a husband who not long ago said to me, "If my wife will do all five of those things, then I'll *think* about changing!"

Moonlight hides some of the rough edges of our lives; but when the sun rises, nothing is left unexposed and the reality testing that takes place is harsh. There is, however, some good news! Things very seldom grow at night. It takes the intensity of the sun to produce nature's changes. The stark realities of our lives often become the seed beds for the new harvest. Facing one's self in relationships, honestly, is the beginning of change. Ben and Carol hit rock bottom, but from that foundation they have made significant progress. They have discovered a new intimacy and how to use it. That discovery was based on the principle I want to share with you in the next chapter on how to join two worlds.

9.

Two Worlds:
Can They Be Joined?

IN A THESAURUS I ran across this note about spelling the word *marriage:* "If you're married, this is an easy word to spell. Just remember, there's an *I* in marriage." This is a cute idea for spelling, but the *I* in marriage may represent the biggest obstacle to the successful relationship.

There is also an *I* in pride. From our earliest experiences as infants, each of us develops an ego and with it a battery of defenses to protect the inner "me" from whatever I judge to be painful. Within each of us is a conflict between two fears—the fear of being known and the fear of being alone. Pride is the mother of my defenses. I want to impress you, to hide from you my faults and defects. I am afraid to let you know me. I'm afraid that if you know me as I do, you won't like me. If you don't like me, then love is not possible. I "put my best foot forward" to solicit your positive responses. This is the courtship game. It has much in common with other human relationship experiences. Pride keeps me at an unknowable distance from others.

Truthfulness reveals my need for others. When I am honest, I admit that I hope to be known, to feel close and accepted by others. This desire brings me to marriage, an institution designed to help me and you to bridge our fears and share the joys and sorrows of life. The oldest reference to the marital conjugal union is the Hebrew verb *to know*. The intimacy of marriage is intended to be a healthy state of self-disclosure, a place to be known.

When a man and woman marry, two worlds are merged. Each world has strengths and weaknesses, good and bad habits, developed and undeveloped resources. This merger is a major undertaking. It does not surprise me that around 45 percent of those who marry divorce. What is astonishing is that 55 percent of the young people who make this demanding decision have the foresight to choose well enough to remain married for life. Divorce statistics are not surprising; marriage success is amazing!

Marriage is like two spaceships in different orbits accidentally meeting and discovering that they have been equipped with the proper interlocking devices which allow them to join resources while in orbit. The odds against such a chance encounter are astronomical. Yet we anticipate that human beings will be able to do this successfully when they choose. What contributes to this successful event? Two people who know themselves well unite physically, mentally-emotionally, and spiritually. This is the key to this book: you cannot try marriage unless you genuinely experience it at these three levels. Anything less is an insufficient experience of the relationship.

Marriage Is a Physical Relationship

The first corner of the marital triangle is the physical one. Knowing each other physically ranks in equal but not superior position with the mental-emotional and spiritual dimensions of marriage.

One can scarcely count the books which have been written about human sexuality. Indeed, since the beginning of the Kinsey research and, more particularly, with the proliferation of the Masters and Johnson data, we have experienced a revolution of sexual information. Regrettably, the people who may need the information most either do not have access to it or are unwilling to read it; in the same period of history unwanted pregnancies and venereal diseases have continued to increase.

I will not attempt to make a portion of this book a sex manual; however, there are four basic elements of the physical relationship we need to examine. They are:

1. A basic self-knowledge.
2. Attraction to your partner.
3. A working understanding of the opposite sex.
4. Essential sexual attitude openness.

I have omitted basic good health in this list. A prerequisite to any effective counseling or psychotherapy is a physical checkup. Marital dysfunction indicates a similar need. However, even severely handicapped individuals with proper support and stimulation can learn to enjoy a healthy physical relationship. Let's look more specifically at these four areas.

A Basic Self-Knowledge

No man or woman should come to marriage without an adequate knowledge of his own physical being. This level of experience should include not only the basic facts about how a body functions but also some ability to verbalize one's feelings about his own anatomy. Having watched the embarrassment on counselees' faces, I know the discomfort a person feels when he must refer to a sexual organ as "my thing" (or a number of other slang words parents have inflicted upon their children). Numerous women have said, while blushing, something about their feelings "down there" (referring to the vaginal area). Every adult needs a basic working knowledge of his own anatomy, including some practice at pronouncing appropriate clinical terms for the body. A therapist may feel empathy for an adult who struggles with embarrassment. Your child is not likely to feel empathy, however. Rather, he will predictably get a negative message about your sexual feeling. Don't let that happen to you or your children.

From my conversations with nonorgasmic women, I must add one further point. No adult should be ashamed of her efforts to know her own body. Many women have experienced a breakthrough with the practice of self-stimulation. A number of helpful resources offered by women describe the techniques fully.[1] Similar books are available for the male reader.[2]

Attraction to Your Partner

A person is unlikely to enjoy a physical relationship with an individual who is unattractive to him. Before you decide that that rules you out, remember that what is attractive differs from person to person. Your partner's appeal to you may not even be physical in nature. For years I have asked husbands and wives what attracted them to each other. Hav-

---

[1] See *Our Bodies, Ourselves,* Boston Women's Health Collective (New York: Simon and Schuster, Inc., 1972) and Lonnie Barbach, *For Yourself* (Garden City, N.Y.: Doubleday & Co., 1975).

[2] See Anthony Pietropinto and Jacqueline Simmenauer, *Beyond the Male Myth* (NY: Quadrangle/New York Times Co., 1977); Bernie Zilbergeld, *Male Sexuality: A Guide to Sexual Fulfillment* (Boston: Little, Brown, and Co., 1978); and James E. Kilgore, *Being a Man in a Woman's World* (Irvine, California: Harvest House, 1975).

ing seen nearly two thousand couples, I have yet to find one partner who was not attracted to his spouse initially by physical appearance. A single feature may be the focus—hair, eyes, breasts, musculature, height—but the senses were attracted in some unique way. Couples have given me a variety of responses to my question, but one couple particularly caught me off guard. A burly ex-navy man replied, "Her tattoo!" When I looked a little puzzled, they both laughed and described how they met in a port city when she was a dancer in a go-go lounge. She had a miniature cobra tattooed on the right side of her buttocks! I did not confirm the report. For most of us, it is something far more ordinary than the unique tattoo that attracts us to our partners.

Most of us will not be initially attracted to a spouse in such an unusual way. (If you have never told your spouse what it was that attracted you, why don't you stop reading now and do that? The book can wait. You will be surprised at the fun and benefit that you both receive from this experience.) Whatever it was, something unique about your marital partner attracted you from an early meeting.

Basic Understanding of the Opposite Sex

If you are a sexual pro, you can skip this section. My experiences dictate a few thoughts on the subject of understanding your spouse. The first idea is that most women have far more sexual capacity than men. There are exceptions, but, as a rule, females can function over a greater period of time and with greater sexual intensity than males. The myth of male sexual supremacy is only that—a myth. Not only are women capable of multiple orgasms whereas men require a period of rest between sexual encounters, their sexual interest rises to a peak between thirty and forty years of age while males reach a zenith in their early twenties. In marriage, women then have a decided edge as the couple matures.

Women generally have been encouraged to explore their feelings and to talk more freely about their sexual needs than males. If you're a man, that gives you two clues. First, the place to build intimacy and initiate sexual pleasure with your wife is in conversation and mental stimulation. Second, your capacity to be sensitive and to share your feelings may be a more important measure of your masculinity than the size of your male organ. I've developed these themes further in chapter 6 of *Being a Man in a Woman's World*.[3]

For women, two words about men: First, games and manipulations do not have long-lasting results in marriage. In spite of the fact that seduction has been suggested as the cure-all for marital ills, I believe that most men will respond only temporarily to being manipulated sexually. "Acting" is not really a convincing sensuous response to a man. While attempts at new sexual behavior require effort before becoming natural, a continuing pretense will add to the distance between you and your man. He may even become less interested in sexual activity—probably just about the time you really decide to enjoy it. It is safe to assert that a man wants most of all to know that a woman is responding to him as a whole being, not simply inducing an involuntary response from his loins.

The second word about men is that many of them need a lot of encouragement to talk openly at a feeling level. Since men are generally taught early expectations about anticipated performance—on the job, in society, and in bed—it becomes difficult for them to acknowledge feelings about or of inadequacy. There are two themes that run through the conversations of husbands that support this idea. One is expressed in the idea of "not letting my family down." Every boy must have been told when he was a child, "Someone is

---

[3] James E. Kilgore, *Being a Man in a Woman's World* (Irvine, California: Harvest House, 1975).

depending on you." Whether it is the responsibility of being the wage earner or the feeling that he "ought" to be *head* of his house, many men carry this weight uneasily. Faced with the idea of "living up to" the expectations of others, few men have the courage to be something different, especially when the fear of failure in the new effort is strong. A wife who understands this struggle may be the greatest boon to personal growth a husband has.

The other aspect of men's imprisonment within themselves is their unwillingness to accept the right to individuality. They are molded by mothers, teachers, wives, vocational expectations, company policy and so on until they literally do not know who they are. The result for many men is the seed of later rebellion. Edmund Berger called it "the revolt of the middle-aged man." When a man finally feels he has given the basics to his wife and children, he often reacts rashly, reaching out for what he may have missed—clothes, a new car, time off for recreation. These symbols of his rebellion are but the outward responses to an inner frustration which has been present for some time—a sense of depersonalization. How much better for a man to learn to assert himself and to express his personhood fully without the necessity of going through this early forties rebelliousness.

Wives, encourage your husband to share his feelings with you. Practice listening. You may soon discover you know him more deeply. In return he will listen more attentively as you share yourself with him.

Essential Openness in Sexual Attitudes

In working with couples who do not function effectively sexually, I have become increasingly aware how many people lack basic sexual information. I will not try to repeat the work which has been done by others in this chapter. Let me recommend for basic reading *A Doctor Speaks on Sexual*

Expression in Marriage by Donald Hastings, M.D.[4] Another
fine book, written from a biblical perspective, is *The Act of
Marriage* by Tim and Beverly La Haye.[5] A list of additional
references is included in the bibliography for this chapter at
the conclusion of the book. Contained in these books is the
kind of basic factual data that is needed from which to practice the attitudinal development I want to describe.

Three concepts about sexuality emerge. If these are prac-
ticed, communication about sexual feelings and a new sense
of intimate sharing will develop. The first is, *be unrestricted!*
That's almost as ridiculous as the command to "be spontaneous." But, I'm willing to show you how to become more
unrestricted or uninhibited.

Let's not worry about the causes of your inhibitions. You
have them, and that's the problem. Begin to rid yourself of
them by acknowledging that you have restrictions that keep
you from being free in your sexual development. These restrictions are not morality; in your marriage relationship
there is no immorality. To accept an inhibition as a negative
block to your personal freedom is the starting point.

Next, let yourself admit that your negative attitude is now
stronger than the positive one you wish to develop. Old
habits are difficult to break and your psyche will need time
to practice the new behavior in order to become comfortable
with it. Don't identify discomfort with failure. It is more
natural to resist change than to allow it. Specifically, give
yourself permission to know sexual facts.

Then, allow yourself enough time to respond to your own
feelings. To feel uninhibited is not equal to becoming free
behaviorally, with no restrictions. Being open within the
context of marriage relationships is not to be equated with
one's public discussion of sexual matters. Each of us has

---

[4] Boston: Little, Brown & Co., 1971.
[5] Grand Rapids: Zondervan Publishing House, 1976.

within himself an indicator of comfort. No one will be able to talk you into doing or saying anything which goes against that basic level of protectiveness within you. However, you can give yourself permission to release the restrictions and enjoy a new sense of freedom about your being. Try it; you'll be glad you did.

The *second* attitude to cultivate is, *be aggressive.* Find out for yourself how your sexual responses feel. Ask questions about your spouse's feelings. Read some articles and books on the subject. Use your right to know. Robert Browning said, "A man's reach should exceed his grasp." To be sexually adult is to control the limits of your own thinking, feeling, speaking, and acting. It is time to accept that responsibility for yourself. No one will help you know what you do not desire. The admonition of the New Testament is, "Ask, and it shall be given you; seek, and you shall find; knock, and it shall be open to you." There is no greater permission or invitation to aggressive behavior than those words.

Third, *be willing to experiment, risk, and grow.* When you free yourself from the past and reach for a full measure of the present, the future will be different. New experiences embody new knowledge and bring new feelings.

Almost twenty years ago in one of my early experiences with an inhibited married couple, I learned something significant. They came in for that appointment tense and struggling with each other. Both acknowledged disappointing sexual life. Gently we explored their feelings. I remember asking them to go home and do certain exercises together. Each of them looked uncomfortable when I suggested the process but both of them agreed to try. What a change when they came back for their second appointment! They were aglow with their new-found sexual feelings. The honeymoon had been reinstituted. What changed them was not my advice. They were willing to experiment and to try new behavior. They found within themselves the resources to begin to experience different feelings. That method still works.

A superb physical and sexual marital experience is not the only indispensable resource for a lifetime of commitment. But it is foundational, and a happy marriage is built on a satisfying sex life.

Marriage Is Also a Mental-Emotional Relationship

A second corner in the marriage triangle is equally important, the mental-emotional arena. It includes both public and private dimensions of the couple's development. Not only must the partners be attracted physically to each other, a genuine pleasure in their shared experiences is needed. This sharing is not limited to aspects of the marriage in which both partners are alike, but also includes the opposite or complimentary elements.

Awareness

The first step in personal growth is awareness of who I am, how I feel, what I think. Marital growth is very similar. I need to be familiar with who you are, how you feel, and what you think—not only to like you personally, but to share with you those things we mutually enjoy. You need to have the same awareness of me. A physical orgasm is an experience every couple should share; but none of us could endure the intensity and sheer delight of that moment on an extended basis. We traffic more frequently in the mini-orgasms of mental and social intercourse than the passions of physical ones.

More marriages fail where people are bored than when they are sexually frustrated. We must have something more than bodies to share with one another. People who stay alive intellectually and emotionally are more likely to develop increasing levels of pleasure together. Their sharing may be enhanced by the differences in their interests. What they read may be less important than the reading activity and taking the time to exchange ideas.

When working with husbands and wives, I often suggest bibliotherapy (a fancy term for using books) as an adjunct to our sessions. My method usually involves the husband's reading one book and the wife another. When they read, I ask them to underline and write in the margins their reactions to the content. When each has finished, I have them exchange books, sharing with each other the most beneficial personal responses. When they read each other's books, I suggest a different color for marking and reactions. This provides the additional stimulation of discussing the differences in their views and ideas. Many couples have indicated the helpfulness of this process in stimulating growth within their marriage, particularly in the improvement of communications patterns.

Varieties of ways exist for couples to gain stimulation. The key to marital benefit is regular sharing. One couple who signed up for a Spanish course at a nearby university said that the class was a positive benefit. The greatest gain for their marriage, however, was not studying the language but the regular time they could spend together in the hour's drive to and from the campus. Now they take a course almost every quarter. Another pair enrolled in separate classes, but used their travel time in the car to talk to each other and to share what each was learning.

Activities which do not require mental preparation may also prompt exchange. Symphony concerts, stage shows, plays, and musicals provide common interest for some couples. Hobbies, community service, sharing athletic events with friends—these are just a few of the sources of stimulation that different individuals may find beneficial for their relationships. Growth reaches higher and higher levels as a couple becomes attuned to each other. Mystery may have its own excitement, but predictability is a much greater comfort to many spouses.

Being aware of each other is a matter of sharing feelings as well as intellectual concepts. In this complex realm, husbands and wives have infinite capacity for being sharpened by emotional exchange. A partner's feelings, explored and known at a given point in the relationship, may change through a new and different series of experiences.

A popular television game show called "The Newlyweds" is based on the ability of the husband or wife to predict how his or her spouse will answer a series of questions. Couples who are confident they know each other are often shocked by the actual responses they receive. Counselors use a similar technique by comparing expectations with actual occurrences in the marriage.

Michelle grew up in a home where she had a strong but passive father. He was quietly in control of much of the family activity. Her mother, on the other hand, was the more volatile, active and apparently aggressive person. When Michelle married Rick, she saw him as an open and straightforward individual. She anticipated being able to share her feelings and being happy with his making the "final decisions." Having always verbally identified with her mother, Michelle thought she would lean on Rick. In counseling with them I reflected to her the similarities I observed between Rick and her mother while her behavior tended to parallel her father's actions.

At first neither of them liked the mirror I was holding up. Slowly, however, each of them began to let go of old assumptions they had held. New depths of feelings were shared in their conversations. As they became aware of new insights in themselves, each was more informed and ready to share with the other.

Awareness is alertness to your partner. It is not mind-reading or crystal-ball gazing. To be alert, cultivate these characteristics: asking, listening, empathizing, remembering, displaying tenderness, seeing, comforting, touching, accompanying, enabling, and respecting. These traits are all part of being aware of your mate.

Assertiveness

A second style of behavior in the deeper mental-emotional relationship is assertiveness. Let's examine this characteristic by contrasting it to aggressiveness. Both are forceful terms, but the use of the self is the distinguishing trait. Aggressive behavior wins, dominates, controls, and places the other as an adversary. Aggressiveness keeps your partner on the defensive in the relationship. Since marital partners are not intended as opponents, this behavior is destructive in most marriages. Assertive behavior, by contrast, gives expression to action, demonstrates strength, uses personal skills, accepts responsibility, channels energy positively, and respects the life-space of those involved. Aggressiveness is domineering; assertiveness is demonstrative but not punitive. Let's illustrate with Michelle and Rick.

As a child, when Michelle heard her parents disagree, there were some code words—expressions which often emerged in conversations. She could recall her mother saying, "If you don't . . . I'm going to leave you." Many things were inserted in the space after *don't,* but her father usually replied, "Go ahead, if that's what you really want to do." Her mother never left home, and Michelle reports her parents are happier now than ever before in their marriage. During one of her arguments with Rick, Michelle heard Rick saying, "If you don't, I'll . . . ." It dawned on her that this was the same pattern her parents had used.

This kind of exchange in a marriage is called conditional

acceptance. This behavior is manipulative. When a partner expresses an "if you don't, then I will . . ." accusation, a negative response is generally returned. The aggressive spouse seeks control by keeping his partner on the defensive. Sentences are characteristically begun with the word *you*. Here are some examples:

You make me mad.

You should have told him. . . .

Why didn't you do it this way?

You always mess things up.

The result of this communication is that the partner feels blamed, attacked or intimidated. An extremely mature person might handle such an opening foray and respond in a way that avoids an argument, but such adeptness is rare.

The assertive person may deal with the same issues. His communication, however, does not place blame on the spouse. Look at the same series of content statements without the negative attacking element present.

I feel angry or I am angry about . . .

I might have said . . . or, It's hard to think quickly in that situation.

I tried it this way and liked the results, or, Are there other ways to attempt that?

I have trouble with that, or, Would you like some help?

The sentences begin with the word *I*. This tends to keep the responsibility of feelings with the person who is speaking. Of course, to be convincing the words must be congruent with the tone expressed.

The assertive person believes in his own rights and responsibilities but does not need to blame, dominate, or manipulate his spouse. Now that Rick and Michelle have learned to think in sentences beginning with *I*, not only do they communicate more effectively, they have fewer but more productive arguments. Positive assertion in communication is the second step to a deepening mental-emotional level of interaction.

Appreciation

The third door to more fully sharing mental-emotional depth is appreciation. Friedrich Nietzsche said: "It is not lack of love but lack of friendship that makes unhappy marriages." More than one couple has told me that the secret to the success of their marriage was their friendship. They appreciated many of the same things in life, and they especially liked each other. From this base each can give and receive support from the relationship.

Here is a subtle test of your similarity to your spouse. Each of you takes a piece of paper and lists twenty people you like and a sentence to explain what particularly impresses you about that person. When you have finished, compare lists. If you have seven or more people on both lists, you have an extremely high degree of similarity. To see how compatible your needs are, take another page and divide it in half. List on the left side what you need from a relationship and on the right side, what you have to offer in a relationship. Compare your spouse's needs list to your resources list and vice versa. Six or more complementary areas shows a strong pattern of compatibility.

Because people are different, some people are attracted and balanced by those who are opposite to themselves. Others feel more secure and identify more easily with a person who is more alike. For this reason it becomes very difficult to talk about universal norms in marriage. But that need not disturb us. Most of us choose friends for reasons we might not understand and continue to relate to those persons even when we recognize our reasons as irrational or even undesirable.

Marriage Is a Spiritual Union

If it is difficult to communicate about the mental-emotional element of marriage, the spiritual dimension becomes a complete quagmire for the majority of couples. Let's try to shed some light in this area.

The triangle of marital parts is like a rare three-cylindered engine. It may roughly function with only one of its cylinders working. The operation is smoother with two working chambers, but the engine was designed to function on three. My own view of man is a wholistic one. Discussing "spiritual" things is only a frame of reference for the purpose of communication. Husbands and wives do not proceed along a one-two-three path from physical attraction to intellectual stimulation to spiritual sharing. Intimacy in marriage is the result of multiple levels of interaction through a variety of experiences. Physical attraction is observable. Couples verbalize much of their mental-emotional partnership. Few couples speak in the third world of sharing, the "spiritual" world, by which I mean the place a man and woman encounter divine reality within themselves and together. Both experiences add to their sharing. Look at two couples.

I first met Bob and Jane early in my practice in Atlanta. I did everything I knew to help them in counseling. They were impatient for results; so was I. When we talked about faith, both of them professed to be religious people. One night I suggested that each of them take hands and silently pray for each other for the next seven nights. Reluctantly, they agreed to try. By the third night each of them "felt closer to each other." Jane said, "Somehow, as each of us tried to open our hearts to God, we drew nearer to each other." When I saw them again, I could tell they had turned a corner in their relationship. Feeling open to God helped them to feel open to one another. This experience did not solve all their problems, but they had tapped an area of resource which has helped them immeasurably.

Ann and Ted were members of the local Episcopal parish. They seemed worlds apart in their marriage. Ted, a young career man who was under a great deal of pressure to achieve, was not really committed to working on the marriage. Ann came for an individual session during a particularly rough time. During the hour she recalled how good she had felt during high school and college; as she put it, "When I talked to God, he really seemed to be listening to me." At the close of our time I suggested an experiment. Ann was to pray for Ted for five minutes every day for the next month. Since loneliness was a major problem for him, I suggested that she make part of her prayer, "Lord, help me to be part of the answer to Ted's loneliness today." Three weeks later Ted came to see me. He was ready to work on their marriage. Ann is convinced the experience of prayer was in large measure a turning point.

Prayer is one expression of the souls of people. Verbalizing feelings of joy or sadness from deep within draws us together in a unique way. Two can become one in spirit through prayer. Other acts of worship together are mystical rituals of the spiritual union. Each has its own particular benefit to an individual couple.

The inner dimension of faith is more, however, than our spiritual ceremonies, public or private. Where two mutually unite in faith, a new bond of hope exists. This joint commitment provides a special cohesiveness in many of the testing incidents in our lives. The shared faith creates a view of life that gives hope. It is no more apparent than in death. When a couple loses a child, the hope of life after death brings comfort. Even in the grief of losing a mate, one can experience an anticipated further reunion in the life to come.

A young physician recently asked me at a lecture, "Isn't all this religious stuff just a placebo? Can you demonstrate what 'spiritual' is in a relationship?" My answer to him was that all psychic data is difficult to demonstrate. The marriage relationship has been the least-researched institution of man, and I cannot prove love in a marriage. I can only show its results. I cannot actually see wind, but I can feel its currents and watch its passing through the trees. The presence of God in a marriage is like that too.

Dr. G. W. Fiske reported a study in the early 1960s that revealed the national average for divorce was one in four marriages. Among active church members, the divorce rate dropped to one in 145 marriages. The old adage, "The couple who prays together stays together" seemed to have some sort of validity.

Here's a proposal. If you and your spouse enjoy a good physical relationship, you have one-third of the possible areas of sharing. If you have a mentally and emotionally stimulating interchange, great. You are two-thirds there. Why not reach for the brass ring? Get all three dimensions going for you. Set up your own experiment of the spiritual reality. You can only gain. This is a prayer for the couple who have not "tried God."

> God, we don't know you on a first-name basis, but we'd like to begin today our conversation with you.
>
> We have found each other and in discovering love have multiplied our individual happiness. Maybe you have been there all along, and we didn't know it. Today we will begin to acknowledge your presence and to be open to all that you may do in our lives. Help us not to miss anything good in our marriage.
>
> We don't know what to expect, but we are ready to start. Thank you for beginning with us. Amen.

Two worlds—can they be joined in one? All of the ideals of marriage point to that union. At our best we do become one. That combined strength is important.

Not long ago I helped my uncle do some remodeling on our house. A certain process required a strong board. He took two pieces of lumber, neither one of which by itself would have been useful in this place in the construction.

Taking some glue and a few nails, he made two boards, which alone could not have held the stress of the load, into a single, fused board strong enough to do the job required. Somehow I see God taking two lives, a man and a woman, neither of whom could have made it alone, to make one solid union. What God brings together, let no man pull apart.

10.

The Balanced Marriage

"THIS IS COLLISION, not merger!" His tone snapped the word, and he glared across the room at his wife. "Don't expect me to compromise my morals to please you!" she retorted.

A marriage counselor is not really a good referee; I cut in on the fight before it escalated further. "Perhaps I can be more helpful if I know what the two of you are debating."

Their personal stylishness belied the anger that overflowed in the marital history. Sylvia was a refined lady when she met John. He was an intelligent, handsome, and rather intriguing man. Married at twenty-six, each brought some maturity to the relationship. Twenty-five years later and with two children in college, they felt themselves needing some rejuvenation in their intimate life. John brought home a "swinger's magazine." Together they looked at the pictures and advertisements. John suggested writing a couple of the "advertisers" in the tabloid "just for fun." Sylvia agreed.

The next step was a letter from an apparently "normal" couple who seemed to have much in common with them.

Discovering a mutual interest in golf, the two couples agreed to meet at a resort midway between their homes. The "new friends" were experienced in mate-swapping. John was immediately attracted to Helen, although Sylvia didn't find Hubert as stimulating. The second night, after several drinks before and during dinner, John and Hubert exchanged keys and bed partners.

John and Sylvia had begun what they called "open" marriage. The results of their sexual permissiveness was an erosion of trust and hope. Sylvia professed her distaste for their three years of swinging. "I didn't like it from the beginning, but what could I do?" she belatedly protested. John accused her of changing her mind. For several weeks their struggle continued in counseling, but ended in divorce.

This couple illustrates a need present in every marriage: to balance the need for each other appropriately against the needs for interaction with others. Sometimes "open" marriage means a good balance; "closed" marriage may mean an imbalance.

George and Nena O'Neill did much to thrust this term into marital discussions when they wrote the book *Open Marriage*.[1] When Ms. O'Neill later wrote *The Marriage Premise,* she had herself been divorced and lived through her eldest son's divorce. She concludes: "This book represents my search for the common ground we all share in marriage, no matter what kind we have. It is my hope that this book will reaffirm for many others those values we have always cherished in human relationships. Marriage still remains that unique relationship which offers us the profound satisfactions and rewards of experience shared with another in love,

---

[1] George and Nena O'Neill, *Open Marriage* (New York: M. Evans & Co., 1972).

commitment, and the excitement that make life a true adventure." [2]

While a sense of growth and open relationships with other adults is an essential ingredient in a healthy marriage, sexual exchanges and extramarital encounters are not the answer. Having seen more than a thousand couples in the counseling office, I can assuredly affirm that sexual fidelity continues to be an essential attribute of most satisfying marriages.

If the terms *open* and *closed* don't describe adequately what we seek, perhaps the dichotomy between *balanced* and *unbalanced* will express the concept.

Two Basic Types of Marriages

Marriages can be divided into styles of complementarity and similarity. Relationships of complementarity are successful when the couple balances their differences. Much like riding a seesaw, each pushes and relaxes as required by the efforts from his partner.

Lawrence and Lola have a complementary relationship. They would not survive otherwise! Lawrence, at forty-seven, is distinguished in appearance by greying sideburns. He is a bank officer, dresses fairly conservatively, and acts with some caution. Lola is typical of the "what Lola wants, Lola gets" theme. Spontaneous and vivacious, she is predictably unpredictable! Usually found trying each new fad, Lola is a constant flutter of activity and expression. An unlikely pair? Yes, but they succeed through balance. His quiet caution complements and restrains her exuberant impulsiveness. Yet her zest for living pulls him from the nest which, though comfortable, often stagnates.

---

[2] Nena O'Neill, *The Marriage Premise* (New York: M. Evans & Co., 1977).

Similarity relationships succeed when the couple's likes and dislikes follow a pattern of support. By sharing, the partners reenforce each other.

Ted and Myrna successfully developed a similarity pattern. They enjoy a number of common pursuits: gourmet cooking, jogging, horticulture, reading, and attending cultural events. They communicate adequately about their mutually enjoyed areas of life. The balance in their relationship comes in the process of choice. Each shares in the wide arena of interests.

When imbalance occurs, the systems couples build fail to function. The *complementarity* system is faulty where the partners do not communicate. Since there is such variety, isolation results quickly when information and excitement isn't transmitted. The *similarity* system fails when either party begins to insist on giving preference to his own interests.

Let me illustrate. When I first met Lawrence and Lola, they were in a transition process. Lola, having gotten her children into school, wanted to begin developing a career. Her interests were in art and musical theater. She had been a cheerleader and enjoyed dancing in high school, but married at eighteen. At thirty-six she considered herself still capable of dancing with a local production group. Initially, her rehearsal schedule presented some changes and adjustment in the patterns for meals and chores. Lawrence objected strenuously to her "neglect" of the children. Lola soon grew tired of the pace but enjoyed being away from home part of the day. In the counseling process, some compromises both in understanding and communication were reached. Lola was able to talk about her satisfaction as a mother and her enjoyment of the role of wife, but expressed other needs. As she developed her additional opportunities for career, she modified her plans, eventually opening an art and theatrical supplies shop. She kept her contacts with a fascinating group of people, and Lawrence assisted in the organization and accounting process at the shop.

Achieving a Balanced Marriage

They dealt with the crisis, and a potential divorce was averted. I saw two ingredients in this process which are useful in many marriages. Lawrence and Lola wanted their relationship to work. They succeeded by using the two commitments of a balanced marriage: they affirmed to each other, first, you are more important to me than any other person in the world; and second, because I love you, I will not only try to be a growing person, I will not knowingly limit your growth.

When these two principles are applied in an atmosphere of honesty, the results are predictably satisfying.

Here's how Lawrence applied them. In our confrontations he began to see that he was attempting to limit Lola's pursuits more because of the inconvenience to him than for substantial disagreement with her goals. As they found ways to compromise, he discovered that he could not only support her, but that they grew closer rather than apart in the process. At first Lola impulsively fought for "her rights" but began to see that she wanted Lawrence's support and help rather than a fight. When she saw that he also wanted what was good for her, finding ways to discuss plans and solicit his advice was supportive rather than controlling.

Balance for Lawrence and Lola meant recognizing, affirming, and encouraging their differences. In doing so, they found some personal satisfaction while each offered the other support. They succeeded by concentrating their energies on the central issues: their love for each other and the resulting positive effect that feeling could produce.

Most marital conflicts can be resolved through this process. Here's a series of questions to guide you when you feel at a loss as to a solution.

How did this impasse develop?

What is the most important result I want from this struggle?

How can I communicate that main point to my mate more effectively?

Does my mate know today that I feel he/she is the most significant person in my life?

How am I growing at this juncture in our marriage?

Could I be limiting his/her growth in this conflict?

What is the worst possible thing that could happen if I don't win this fight we are having? Can I live with that result? What underlies my fears about this?

A balanced marriage incorporates our needs for each other and our needs for others. The function of such balance is easily seen in the diversity of pairing like Lawrence and Lola. It may be more difficult to distinguish in the similarity patterns.

Ted and Myrna were so much alike they bored each other. In their attempts to share with one another, dependency became the predominant characteristic of the marriage. The similarity pattern can bring too much conformity and too little variety. A carbon copy adds nothing to an original; so a spouse who is just like the mate is not beneficial. When two people agree on everything, one of them is unnecessary.

Without recognizing their dependency, both Ted and Myrna were limiting themselves, perhaps voluntarily, but nevertheless destructively, by their expectations of each other. Early in my sessions with them, Ted said, "I would really like to try hunting, but Myrna wouldn't like being alone." As we examined that statement, he began to see that he was using her as an excuse not to experiment with new interests. Each feared disapproval from the other; each attempted to do those things which pleased the other. When doubt existed, omission was the simplest course.

Thus as they developed too much need for each other, resentment built in each of them. The discomfort erupted when Myrna accused Ted of not enjoying a performance she chose for them. Implied in the accusation seemed to be the idea he had not enjoyed being with her. When Ted said he had not particularly been impressed with the artist, Myrna heard rejection of herself.

Using the evaluation questions listed earlier, I helped the two of them see again what their marital goals were. When they examined the patterns of their behavior, the destructive dependency was obvious. Today they are still sharing most things, but their new sense of balance includes rather than excludes others from the relationship.

The unbalanced relationship in the similarity pattern creates dependency. Hostility is the natural reaction. It may be expressed in active or passive defensiveness. In the complementarity pattern lack of balance creates distance and isolation. Distrust and antagonism breed in this emotional soil like mosquitoes in stagnant water. Angry verbal outbursts result.

The balanced marriage is a composite of self, spouse, and others. When others divide spouse and self, the result is dangerous. In lectures I illustrate this "cry-for-help" pattern by writing the words on a blackboard this way: Self, Others, Spouse equals S.O.S. (Help!). When others are totally excluded, the self and the spouse tend to form a single *s* which is much too limited for growth. The "SSO" of Self, Spouse, and Others can also be translated Satisfaction, Stimulation, and Openness—three ingredients which characterize success in marriage.

11.

A Month for Your Marriage

I HAVE SUGGESTED that marriage is a "do-it-yourself kit."
This chapter describes a plan to revitalize your relationship
in just thirty days. If that seems like a major project, I simply challenge you to try it. See what happens for you and
your mate!

The exercises are divided into four sets of seven. For
seven days you concentrate on yourself and engage in self-
discovery. Sidney Jourard has suggested we know ourselves
only as we disclose what we know to others. You spend the
second seven-day period sharing with your spouse. The next
seven days you return to self-disclosure, and the final week
is again for sharing. The last two days are for a couple exchange and evaluation.

Before you read the exercises, let me suggest that the two
of you discuss the prospect. If you agree you'd like to do this,
mark your calendar to begin on the first Saturday available.
The advantage of beginning on the weekend comes when
you can conclude the thirty-day period on another weekend.

The last two days will require more time than the first twenty-eight do.

In order to benefit as fully as possible, you will need to set aside fifteen minutes daily. Some couples have discovered they can really get involved with an exercise and talk easily for an hour. One eager couple talked from 11:00 P.M. through to 7:00 A.M. nonstop! Sometimes a satisfying and stimulating marital conversation is like eating one potato chip—it's difficult to stop! For most of us the investment of time in marital exchanges will pay superb dividends.

Two final suggestions: To record your feelings and ideas, you may use this book or you may choose to secure a separate notebook for recording your responses. Second, as you look at the calendar, you may want to plan the last two days as a retreat for the two of you. Travel is not necessary. Many hotels now offer 24- to 48-hour "escape weekends" for couples in the local area. The advantages of getting away are numerous: time for discussion, a break in the living pressures, absence of tasks or interruptions for an extended period, and the joy of being served and entertained by others.

May I wish you two a happy adventure? If you pursue these exercises vigorously, you will have different perspective in a month and your marriage will have grown. Bon voyage!

SELF-DISCLOSURE EXERCISE NO. 1

Know Thyself First!

Polonius, in the play *Hamlet,* is given this line by William Shakespeare: "To thine own self be true; and it must follow as day follows night, thou canst not then be false to any man."

Self-disclosure is the process of looking at that which is known to me but hidden from others whether deliberately or inadvertently. This exercise focuses on who you are. It may be helpful to consider some of the things others think you are but, for the most benefit, look squarely at the core of who you are. Fill in the blanks twenty times after the words, "I am : . . ." Then examine the list and go beyond twenty or revise the things you have written.

Here are a few examples:

I am a man (or woman).

I am a wife, mother (husband, father).

I am a sensitive (insensitive?) person.

I am someone who depends on others' ideas or opinions.

I am a person with a sarcastic streak.

Now it's your chance. Who are you?

1. I am . . .

2. I am . . .

3. I am . . .

4. I am . . .

5. I am . . .

6. I am . . .

7. I am . . .

8. I am . . .

9. I am . . .

10. I am . . .

11. I am . . .

12. I am . . .

13. I am . . .

14. I am . . .

15. I am . . .

16. I am . . .

17. I am . . .

18. I am . . .

19. I am . . .

20. I am . . .

SELF-DISCLOSURE EXERCISE NO. 2

Mirror, Mirror on the Wall

Do you remember the wicked queen in Snow White? She asked her mirror daily, "Who is the fairest of them all?" She was upset when she didn't get the answer she wanted. We can manipulate life's reflections to us just the way the queen did, or, we may learn from what we see in the mirrors that people hold up for us. "Feedback"—what others say to us in words or in actions—mirrors the impressions they have of us. I've suggested a few names to get you started. Try for at least ten significant people in your life; if you can do more, that's great. Look deeply; what you see can help you.

1. My husband/wife sees me as . . .

2. My child/children see me as . . .

3. My employer/employees see me as . . .

4. My religion leader (pastor, priest, rabbi) sees me as . . .

5. My neighbor sees me as . . .

6. My close friend sees me as . . .

7. My brother/sister sees me as . . .

8. My parents see (saw) me as . . .

9. My lover sees me as . . .
     etc.

SELF-DISCLOSURE EXERCISE NO. 3

Emergency—Escape with the Essentials!

What do you consider—besides people—to be the essentials of your life? Imagine hearing the word "Fire!" and having just a few minutes to take a few things and evacuate your home. Many things are valuable, but can be replaced. What possessions do you treasure? List ten items quickly. As you think about them, what can you learn about yourself?

Some examples might be:

> Picture of my parents (deceased)
> Coin or stamp collection
> Favorite art piece or antique
> Record collection
> Jewelry, etc.

In an emergency, I would take:

SELF-DISCLOSURE EXERCISE NO. 4

Animal Kingdom—Where Do I Identify?

It is a revealing experience for members of my Personal Growth Program to do this exercise. Each person is asked to assign to every other member of the group the name of an animal whose characteristics are similar. The person need not look like the animal but may remind you by his words, actions, or reactions to others of that animal.

When you have tried this for at least five other people such as those we listed in exercise 2, then pick an animal for yourself. Ask yourself why you chose those particular characteristics for your own animal.

For instance, your father may be like a bear—growling, reclusive, and at times angry and frightening. Your wife may be like a mother hen—clucking solicitously after her chicks or impatiently waiting for the eggs to hatch.

You could be a busy beaver, an ostrich who hides his head from frightening things, or a deer—beautiful but skittish of strangers. Try it; you'll be surprised at the results.

SELF-DISCLOSURE NO. 5

The Academy Award

Each year the movie world gathers to honor its top stars, directors, artists, and technicians. Let's imagine that you can create a category and receive an award. In what picture would you star, direct, or participate? What award would you receive?

Here are some examples; The movie, "Gone with the Wind" and the award for leading actor, Rhett Butler—indifference personified.

Or, a made-up title such as "You Can't Go Home" and the award, best supporting actress for your relationship to your husband.

Or, "Man of La Mancha" for dreaming "The Impossible Dream," etc.

Be creative. Try your hand at an award.

SELF-DISCLOSURE EXERCISE NO. 6

Six Weeks to Live—How?

To experience this exercise fully, you'll need to imagine that you have just returned from your physician's office. After exhaustive testing and numerous consultations he has concluded that you have only six weeks to live. Because of the nature of your illness, you will not have diminished physical capacity until the final day of your life. You can do anything you choose during the next forty-two days. How would you like to live them?

Write your reactions in your notebook or in the space available here.

SELF-DISCLOSURE NO. 7

Do You Know Where Your Money Goes?

This exercise is designed to help you look at the ways you invest yourself through the money you spend. If you manage most of the family's money, this may represent a broader effort. If you consider only a personal income, salary, or allowance, the same directions apply. Start by listing your weekly or monthly expenditures. You may wish to divide them into larger categories such as shelter, including home, utilities, etc.; food and outside entertainment; clothing; auto or travel expenses; insurance; credit unions savings; investments; charitable contributions, etc.

Don't make this a major mathematical effort. Work in rough estimates. When you have completed listing all the expenses, look at the amounts spent in terms of the percentage of your money available. For example, if your house or apartment takes one-half of your total earnings, how do you feel about that? Is your present car worth 25 percent of your income?

The important goal of this exercise is that you see for yourself where your life energies are being invested.

You have now concluded week one of a Month for Your Marriage. Let me suggest that you put away your notes from this week or paper-clip this part of the book together. Don't look back at what you've written or share this with your spouse during the next seven days. The coming week is designed for the two of you to talk to each other rather than to write your responses. You will share this first week's work later in the month.

For the next week you'll need at least fifteen minutes together each day. Plan to have an uninterrupted period in a private place where you can talk freely. Some couples have tried this series of exercises just before bed, but they have discovered each of them is too tired to get the most from the time spent. You may be a "night couple;" if so, your experience may be different. If you are "day people," plan your time for early evening.

SHARING EXERCISE NO. 1

I Remember You Then

Each of you share what you remember about your initial impressions of each other. It may be the first time you met or your first date.

Some couples find it helpful to begin the exercise with the sentence "I remember you then as . . . " Fill in the blank. Here are some ideas about deepening your exchange. What attracted you most to each other? What attracts you now? How have your feelings changed since that early impression?

Looking back often produces a change in the way we view the present.

SHARING EXERCISE NO. 2

Before I Was Twelve I Met . . .

For this period of sharing concentrate on the most influential persons in your life before you were twelve. Choose one to three people and describe them to each other. Talk about the reasons you selected these individuals. Be sure to describe the characteristics which influenced you.

Here are some examples: "I remember visiting my grandfather. He was always a happy and playful man. I often think of the twinkle in his eye." Or, "When I was nine I had a teacher who encouraged me to try the piano. I had the feeling she believed in me, not just my talent." And, "I think of my Little League coach. He taught me discipline. That has probably influenced me more than I realize."

Enjoy these moments from your childhood. Cherish the past and use it to enhance today together.

SHARING EXERCISE NO. 3

Memories of High School—Wow!

Look together at your years after grade school and before graduation from high school. Choose one or two of the happiest times of that period and share them with each other.

Sample responses might go like this: Sally said "When I was elected Homecoming Queen, it was the happiest night of my life. I remember the feeling of being beautiful as I sat on the back seat of a convertible and rode around the football field." Matt hesitated at first, but finally told Sally, "When I was in high school, I accepted Christ as my Savior. I was part of a group of new Christians. We carried our Bibles to school and identified with each other. I remember that as one of the happiest times of my life."

From those two examples your mind will undoubtedly be triggered into your own high school memories. Share some of those with each other now.

SHARING EXERCISE NO. 4

Life's Most Embarrassing Moments

Think primarily of your premarital years. From your experiences, share with each other one or two of life's most embarrassing times. You may have a few laughs or some tears. Many couples discover that they had never told each other such an interesting or frustrating experience.

Mary told Tom about singing from an illuminated stage in a big performance. Her costume was rather thin. She learned after the show that she was a rather intimate shadow against the lighted background.

Tom remembered his first senior prom. He forgot to buy his date a corsage, and she was the only girl there without flowers. A friend pulled him aside and chided him at the prom.

What will the two of you share with each other?

SHARING EXERCISE NO. 5

Touch Me Gently

For the first four days of this week we have used verbal exchanges to stimulate sharing. Today the modality is non-verbal. I'll describe how you can best do the exercise. You will need two straight chairs which should be placed comfortably close to each other and turned so that you can sit down and face each other. You should be able to put your hands easily on each other's shoulders.

Each of you will do the exercise without speaking. Decide first who will begin. Be seated. Both close your eyes. The first partner will gently, with fingertips, explore the neck, head and face of the second partner. Take time, imagining yourself as a person without sight, discovering how your partner's features are shaped. You will be using your fingertips for "sight" in this exercise. Gently explore the face, hairline, and ears to build a mental picture of your partner. When the first partner has concluded a slow and sensitive discovery, let him return his hands to his lap. The second partner then explores the first partner's face, head, ears, and neck. Both of you keep eyes closed during the entire segment of touching.

When each of you has experienced both touching and being touched, open your eyes. Talk first about what you physically felt in the features of your partner's head and face. Then talk about your inner feelings while doing this exercise.

There are no "right" and "wrong" experiences or feelings. Whatever you sense, share it openly. Bob and Jean told me they felt closer than they had ever been when they did this exercise. Jean said, "In intercourse our bodies are joined.

With my eyes closed I felt my inner being touching Bob's. It was a beautiful experience."

If you will allow yourself to relax, take a few deep breaths, and be in touch with your own feelings, you will discover a wonderfully stimulating exchange.

SHARING EXERCISE NO. 6

Gifts to Remember

Occasions when we give each other gifts are often memorable. Today's exercise is built on those times. Think about some of the things you have given each other. Do not limit yourself to birthday, anniversary, or Christmas gifts. A special "I love you" gift may be recalled too.

Think about the things you have received from your partner. Today share with each other one or two of the most significant experiences in your giving and receiving gifts.

SHARING EXERCISE NO. 7

The Best Vacation I Ever Had

Today I'd like for the two of you to focus on vacation experiences. What was your best "holiday" trip? Or perhaps your most memorable "time out" period involved something other than travel. Discuss thoroughly what makes your memory special.

Here are some sample experiences: Shirley talked about a camping trip just four miles from home. She and Frank really enjoy the outdoors together. "We took a week in the fall while the leaves were turning. I think back on that as a turning point in our lives." Barbara remembered a business trip to Europe when John later joined her for a bicycling vacation. "It was so different; we had never done anything like that in our lives. It was a risk we took and got a happy reward."

What vacation times do you two remember? Talk it over today.

You have completed two weeks of working to understand yourself and your spouse. By now you are no doubt getting in touch with some new feelings and perhaps sensing some different ways of thinking about your marriage.

The third week is devoted to another period of self-discovery. Writing down your thoughts for this week is essential. You may again use the space provided here or work in a separate notebook.

SELF-DISCLOSURE EXERCISE NO. 8

A Moment of Privacy—Look at Me!

Today's assignment is to read your notes from the first week's exercises. Compare your feelings about what you wrote in week one and how you reacted to sharing feelings with your spouse in week two. Write today about what is happening to you in this process. Are you seeing any directions or trends in your thinking? Are your feelings about yourself or your spouse changing? Write at least a paragraph about yourself and another one about your relationship to your spouse.

Need some examples? Maggie wrote, "I'm beginning to sense how separately Ralph and I have been functioning. We've simply drifted apart." Ralph wrote: "I've learned that I'm lonely. I've been thinking about protecting her from my worries. In sharing with Maggie I've felt better about us. I find her somehow stronger than I thought she was. I don't know why."

Write some honest comments about your thoughts and feelings. Talk to yourself on paper. You may discover the same thing that the philosopher Sam Jones did: "How do I know what I'm thinking until I see what I've said?"

SELF-DISCLOSURE EXERCISE NO. 9

Secrets—Do They Tell Me Something?

Think today about the things—ideas, events, or fears—that you have not shared with your spouse. You may not have verbalized these things to another person. They are your "secrets." Have you thought about why you are keeping those particular concerns private? You may have good reasons.

Look at what you've written. Ask yourself about them. This exercise is not designed to force you to talk to your partner. Do the exercise well. If you are uncomfortable with what you've written, tear the page out of the book or your notebook and throw it away. Don't let yourself off the hook by saying, "I have no secrets." Every mental house has a private room or a locked closet. Look there.

SELF-DISCLOSURE EXERCISE NO. 10

Why Am I Doing This?

Concentrate today on your major life assignments. How do you make your living? If you are employed, consider your job, occupation, or professional designation. If you are not employed outside the home, choose a title for what you do such as "homemaker," "child management specialist," "household executive" or whatever seems appropriate. Ask yourself what are the most significant and satisfying factors in this life assignment. What elements are the most discouraging and unfulfilling? Write your comments here or in your notebook.

SELF-DISCLOSURE EXERCISE NO. 11

Freedom: If I Weren't Married, I Would . . .

This exercise is not to encourage you to leave each other! What I want you to do is to list and describe the interests you might pursue if you were free of the obligations and commitments of marriage.

George wrote, "If I didn't have to provide for a family, I'd buy a sailboat and live in the Bahama Islands." Muriel said, "I would go back to school. I've always wished I were a doctor." These are just examples of types of ideas.

Go ahead; it won't hurt you to delineate what else you might do with your life. Most of us do what we really choose.

SELF-DISCLOSURE EXERCISE NO. 12

My Fears: I Wish I Could Tell You

Today we explore fears—the unspoken controls on much of our behavior. I fear being known by you; you might reject me. I fear more the isolation of never being known and accepted by another person. Can you express your fears through writing in your notebook or here on this page?

Brad wrote in his notebook: "I'm afraid Susan will see me as weak. I'm afraid not to be a success; how could she live with a man who failed?" Sharon wrote, "I'm afraid of my anger. Sometimes I get so mad I think I could kill him."

What do you fear? What might you say to your spouse or someone else if you felt free enough to disclose it?

SELF-DISCLOSURE EXERCISE NO. 13

I Wish I Could Change Me

Look at yourself in the light of the exercises we have done so far. Now list two or three things you would like to change about yourself—physically, emotionally, socially, or spiritually. Write about why you wish to make these changes. Take your time; this is a most important phase of the process.

Martin, who did this exercise in a group, wrote, "I don't want to be 'fat and happy' any more." He lost forty pounds! Kathy wrote, "I wish I had larger breasts; I would feel better about myself." She later discussed this wish with a physician and with her husband. As a result, she had cosmetic surgery and looks quite different today!

What would you like to change about yourself? Write it down today.

SELF-DISCLOSURE EXERCISE NO. 14

I Wish I Could Change You

What you did yesterday for yourself, do today about your spouse. If you could do so, what items in your spouse's life would you change? Make a list on this page or in your notebook of the things you might ask your partner to change. Irritating habits, basic conflicts, or undeveloped talents are a few categories to consider.

Focus on your list. Evaluate how important these things are to you. You need not show these to your spouse.

You have concluded the third week of a Month for Your Marriage. There are seven sharing exercises and a two-day summary experience still ahead of you.

These last seven sharing exercises are designed to stimulate interaction and conversation between you. All of the skills you've tried before will be employed in the week's work.

SHARING EXERCISE NO. 8

Who Are You?

To expedite your sharing today, each of you should take a separate piece of paper and on it number from one to ten. In the time you share today, each of you will ask this question ten consecutive times. When your partner asks you who you are, you are to give a different but true response each time. Each of you should answer ten times consecutively. When you ask the question, write down your partner's answers on your sheet.

Some people concentrate on functions, such as "I am an engineer" or "I am a model." You may also want to think about words that describe who you are by making such statements as, "I am a person who feels empathetically" or, "I am someone who likes the outdoors." After each of you has responded to the question and written down ten answers, exchange the sheets. Look at your answers which your partner has written down. Renumber them from 1 to 10 in order of their significance to you. When both of you have done this, read the corrected list and discuss your feelings about the exercise.

SHARING EXERCISE NO. 9

What Can I Give You?

Yesterday you learned the format you will use for today and tomorrow. On a separate sheet write the answers to the question "What can I give you?" that you will ask your spouse ten times. Each time he will give you a true but different response. When both of you have finished, again renumber your answers in priority and discuss your feelings about the responses you gave and those you got.

Remember that you may ask for specific things such as "a new shirt" or "money." Some people ask for "love" or "time alone." Be creative and you'll enjoy this exercise.

SHARING EXERCISE NO. 10

What Can You Give Me?

Notice the difference in yesterday's question, "What can *I* give *you?*" and today's query, "What can *you* give *me?*" Use the same process of asking for ten true but different answers. Write them down as your partner responds. After you have rearranged in priority order the answers you gave, discuss them together.

What reactions do you have to your view of the resources you offer in your marriage? How do you feel about your spouse's "gifts" which you wrote down? What are you feeling about the changes in order the two of you made in your lists? Freely discuss the implications with each other.

SHARING EXERCISE NO. 11

Our Strengths

In today's exercise you will work together. Write in the space below this paragraph or on a separate sheet at least five strengths you have as a couple. Think of these as your assets.

Consider those things that are the result of your coming together. Don't overlook your children, your physical looks (are you together a handsome pair?), your shared beliefs or opinions, your interests and hobbies in common, or the balance you derive in certain areas together.

Beth and John said, "We both enjoy reading and can add to most conversations because of what we have read." Carol and Ed added: "We really enjoy being together. We would be good friends even if we weren't married. We really like each other."

You get the idea. Explore with each other what your strengths are. Find the most positive way to express them. Five is the minimum; go much further if you like.

SHARING EXERCISE NO. 12

Tell Me My Weaknesses Lovingly

Share with each other today by talking about at least two areas you feel your spouse should consider for improvement. It may help to begin by saying, "I think you would be a happier person if . . ." and filling in the sentence. Another way to approach this arena is through this sentence: "When I listen to you, I hear. . . ."

One wife said to her husband, "When I listen to you, I hear your unhappiness with your job. I want you to know I'm with you all the way. If you need to quit, go ahead." A husband said, "I think you would be happier if you felt you could say no to your sister. It hurts me to see you being used."

Don't shrink from this exercise just because it may be difficult. Sensitive and honest comments, lovingly related, build intimacy in a marriage. The unspoken feelings block our growth.

SHARING EXERCISE NO. 13

Look at Our Home—What Does It Say?

Today, I want the two of you to walk through your apartment, house, or trailer—whatever you call home—and look carefully at what you see. Look at different rooms. Where do you see yourself in the choice of furnishings, appointments, or arrangement?

Husbands tend to "cop out" on this exercise by saying "The home is hers; she can do with it what she wants." That isn't fully true. Look for ways you have or have not expressed yourself in the elements of your physical living.

Talk to each other as you go from room to room. The exercise could dissolve into a discussion of taste or furniture arrangement. It may lead to an extended discussion if you pursue it thoroughly.

SHARING EXERCISE NO. 14

If I Were Divorced, I Would . . .

Today's exercise may be extremely critical in leading to
the conclusion of your Month for Your Marriage. What I
want you to do is to tell each other how life would be different if you were divorced from each other. In a self-disclosure
exercise I asked you to think about and write down some
thoughts on what you would do if you weren't married. This
may be a time when you can share some of those ideas. How
would your life change if you were not together?

Discuss thoroughly your feelings about the situation suggested. Remember, you or your spouse may experience a
valid feeling which you may not choose to put into action.

Ron said to Helen: "I feel as if I could live as well without you, but I do not choose to do so." Simply because you
examine an idea or a feeling does not necessarily mean you
will act on it.

Talk fully about your feelings. You need not fear those
feelings and ideas you have expressed and discussed.

SHARING EXERCISE NO. 15

Till Death Do Us Part

When you began these exercises, I suggested that you plan a weekend away to conclude the experiences. I hope the two of you can have at least an overnight where you can share this experience and the final evaluation.

This exercise will require at least an hour, and I want to be explicit about how to do it. We are dealing with the subject of death as the title implies. Decide first who will "play dead." That person will lie down on the floor or on a bed. The other spouse should sit near the head of the person on the bed or floor preferably out of the line of vision. It is best for both partners to keep their eyes closed during the exercise.

The spouse who is "alive" is to do two things: first, he is to imagine himself reading aloud an obituary from the newspaper about his "dead" spouse. The obituary should include an imaginary cause of death, date of death, address, employment, and the survivors of the deceased. Second, you are to fantasize yourself at a memorial or funeral service giving a eulogy about your deceased spouse. Assume you will have the strength to do this. If you should shed tears, it would be understood. As best you can, try now to verbalize your feelings about having lived with this person for the number of years you have been married. Since this is a personal eulogy, you may express feelings about how you see your life changing.

When the first partner has concluded his eulogy, you should swap places and the second speaker should go through the imaginary obituary and memorial eulogy. This is not an easy exercise. Please don't cheat yourself of its benefits by failing to take it seriously.

After each of you has spoken, discuss your feelings and

reactions to this experience. Talk about whether or not you would eventually remarry and why or why not. Talk about your reactions to your spouse's comments in the fantasized eulogy.

Take plenty of time to explore with each other. Open your feelings as much as possible. This can be a most significant experience of sharing.

SHARING EXERCISE NO. 16

What I Have Discovered This Month

If you began your exercises on a Saturday, this thirtieth day will be Sunday. Whether you were on that schedule or not, you are concluding a very probing and intensive self-exploration and disclosure experience. To begin your summary, find a place where each of you can be alone and write a paragraph or two about what you have experienced in the past twenty-nine days. When you have finished that, write a paragraph about what you think your spouse has experienced. Finally, try to summarize in a paragraph the present state of your relationship.

When both of you have finished writing, exchange what you have written and read it in silence. Now talk it over.

What insights have come to you? Have you experienced any change in your relationship? Do you have some new or renewed goals for your future?

Couples who courageously share with each other have the greatest opportunity for intimacy and growth within their marriages. Happiness is the result of such sharing.

As a result of working on this book I wrote ten ideas about couple-happiness. I have called them the Beatitudes for Courageous Couples.

1. Happy is the couple who have discovered in each other a challenging satisfaction; they will constantly offer reassurance without being asked for it.

2. Happy is the couple who have shared a deep sorrow together; they will never be totally alone in the face of crisis.

3. Happy is the couple who know themselves well enough to tell each other they are able to live independently of each other, but do not choose to do so; they will not fear the meaning of their absences from each other.

4. Happy is the couple who have tasted enough of love to have a lifelong addiction; for them intimacy has begun but will never end.

5. Happy is the couple whose love is strong enough to be shared with others; life can never be empty for them.

6. Happy is the couple who risk giving each other loving honesty; they will never have to fear what another person knows about them.

7. Happy is the couple whose faith in each other brings hope and encouragement to other couples; they will be spoken of enviously as "truly happily married."

8. Happy is the couple who finds joy in the love other couples feel for each other; they will not fear for the strength of their own union.

9. Happy is the couple who so live their love for each other that all gossip and rumors about them will be

unbelievable to those who hear; their marriage will be a living expression of commitment.

10. Happy is the couple whose faith in God is experienced personally and conjointly; for that couple's life will always be filled with surprises and will have no unsolvable mysteries.

A Month for Your Marriage is designed to bring you to this kind of happiness. May the two of you be closer today than you were yesterday, but not as close as you will be tomorrow.

12.

More Self-Help Suggestions

IN MY COUNSELING OFFICE, after concluding an initial five-session evaluation process for all couples, I try to make some initial recommendations for each couple's progress. Three styles of help have emerged: (1) traditional psychotherapy, which may involve individual or couple sessions; (2) the therapeutic-educative group which we refer to as the Personal Growth Program (for individuals) and the Marriage Enrichment Program (for couples) ; and (3) self-help programs.

Self-help for couples uses a professional counselor in much the same role as that of a coach in an athletic contest. The counselor makes suggestions and talks about alternatives but is not actually in the game itself. In this chapter I want to share some of the techniques you may find helpful in your work on your marriage.

In severe marital conflicts or in a crisis, I suggest you seek professional help. A good source to locate a reputable and trained marriage and family counselor is The American

Association of Marriage and Family Counselors, 225 Yale Avenue, Claremont, California 91711 (714) 621-4749.

Following professional therapy or for useful explorations into your marriage, the following additional techniques will be helpful.

Reading to Improve Your Marriage

Don't just read a book! Think about what kind of help or information you wish from it. Select your sources and discuss your reading together.

I regularly suggest one book for a husband to read but a different one for his wife. Keep a pen or pencil at hand. As you come to a thought or an idea you like, underline it or write a comment in the margin. Note the things you agree with and also mark the passages you cannot accept. You may find some you don't even understand!

An American minister told this story on a German theologian. One day while they were both in the same city to speak at a conference together, the minister reached for a copy of the theologian's book and turned to a particular page. He asked the author to read the page and tell him what he meant by what he had written there. After thoughtfully reading the page, the theologian puffed on his pipe and finally answered, "When I wrote it, it was wonderful. Now it is nonsense!" Even the author can be critical of what he tried to say. You should be too.

Occasionally I'll ask couples to keep a "My Idea" notebook as they read. When the author sparks something in you, write, "His idea was . . . , but my idea is . . . ," and then express what you feel on the page. Read it to your partner; he or she may have a different idea yet!

As suggested in chapter 9, when partners read two different books, it is a good practice to swap books after the first partner has finished. Each of you should tell the other about the feelings and ideas stimulated by your reading. When you read a book your spouse has read, use a different color pen or pencil. Write your own comments in the margin. That book can now serve as a catalyst for discussion between you.

Here are eleven titles which lend themselves nicely to this process. You can add others.

1. *Letters to Karen* and *Letters to Philip* by Charlie Shedd (Nashville: Abingdon Press, 1965; New York: Doubleday & Co., Inc., 1968).
2. *Why Am I Afraid to Tell You Who I Am?* by John Powell (Niles, Ill.: Argus Communications, 1969).
3. *Fully Human, Fully Alive* by John Powell (Niles, Ill.: Argus Communications, 1976).
4. *Being a Man in a Woman's World* by James E. Kilgore (Irvine, Calif.: Harvest House Publications, 1975).
5. *Letters on Life and Love* by James E. Kilgore.
6. *The Act of Marriage* by Tim and Beverly LaHaye (Grand Rapids: Zondervan Publishing House, 1976).
7. *Habitation of Dragons* by Keith Miller (Waco, Tex.: Word Books, 1970).
8. *Your Erroneous Zones* by Wayne Dyer (New York: Funk & Wagnalls, 1976).
9. *No-Fault Marriage* by Marcia Lasswel and N. Lobsenz (New York: Doubleday & Co., Inc., 1976).
10. *The Mirages of Marriage* by Don D. Jackson and William Lederer (New York: W. W. Norton, 1968).

Another type of reading couples can do is for one partner to read out loud while the other listens. At the conclusion of each chapter they discuss their feelings and ideas.

Four couples I know have formed a reading club. They

meet every other week to discuss a book they've all read. Each couple takes turns leading the discussion about the book under consideration.

Reading has many variations. I have mentioned these few to stimulate your own ideas. As an author, one of my greatest satisfactions is to hear from a reader with a new idea on the use of books in strengthening marriages.

Tapes to Share

The popularity of cassette tapes has made them a ready tool for couples to use in self-improvement pursuits. This is especially true for the couple who travels by car on vacation trips or in the course of work. One inventive couple turned their daily commuter trip into the city into a 45-minute period of marriage growth. Each morning they listened to a tape as they rode into the city. After thinking about the concepts during the day, they discussed their reactions and ideas on their return trip to the suburbs.

When I visited in Korea, a military chaplain told me how he and his family exchanged tapes by mail in order to keep their Mormon "evening at home" while he was away.

An interesting experience in premarital counseling occurred for me when I met with a young lady whose fiancé was in South America on a business assignment. Through a series of taped questions and free association responses, they completed a fairly thorough counseling process prior to their wedding when he returned home on vacation.

Many of the similar uses to reading apply and will not be repeated. Here are some suggestions of tapes from which couples could benefit by listening:

1. Tim La Haye, "How to Be Happy Though Married"
2. Charlie Shedd, "Fun Family Forum"

3. James E. Kilgore, "Dimensions of Personal and Marital Growth"
4. Bruce and Hazel Larson, "Building a Christian Marriage"
5. Floyd Anderson, "Attaining Intimacy in Marriage"
6. Beryl and Noam Chernick, "Sexual Communication in Marriage"

(For information on obtaining these tapes, contact Dr. James E. Kilgore, Northside Counseling Center, 204 Northside Medical Center, 275 Carpenter Drive, N.E., Atlanta, GA 30328.)

Of course, listening together or discussing the tapes which both of you hear is the most helpful use of audio resources.

Self-Help Marriage Programs

A number of groups bringing couples together for marriage enrichment have come into existence in the seventies. One of the finest is that founded by Dr. David and Dr. Vera Mace of Winston-Salem, N.C. It is simply called The Association of Couples for Marriage Enrichment, 459 S. Church Street, P.O. Box 10596, Winston-Salem, N.C. 27108.

Apart from groups led by professionals as part of their counseling practice, some resources for couples exist in the form of courses or weekend experiences.

Among them are:

1. Interpersonal Communication Program, Inc.
   300 Clifton Avenue
   Minneapolis, MN 55403
2. Institute in Basic Youth Conflicts
   Box 1
   Oakbrook, IL 60521

3. Marriage Encounter
   5305 West Foster Avenue
   Chicago, IL 60630

Additional information is available from the Family Ministry Department, Sunday School Board, Southern Baptist Convention, 127 Ninth Avenue North, Nashville, TN 37234; also from the National YMCA, Family Communication Skill Center, 350 Sharon Park Drive, Menlo Park, CA 94025. Another source is the Family Home Evening Program distributed through the Chruch of Jesus Christ of Latter Day Saints, 1999 West 17th South, Salt Lake City, UT 84104. The Reform Church in America and the United Methodist Church provide Marriage Communication Labs, P.O. Box 1986, Indianapolis, IN 46206.

Couples might also be interested in a taped program entitled "Growth Counseling: Part One, Enriching Marriage and Family Life" by Howard and Charlotte Clinebell, which is available through Abingdon Press, 201 Eighth Avenue South, Nashville, TN 37203.

Original Programming

The most constructive self-help programs are those couples create. I've enjoyed hearing reports of long weekends couples planned for themselves. A variety of settings which run the gamut from luxury hotels to state parks for outdoor camping have been used as escapes for special times of intimacy and communication.

Any plan which the two of you negotiate and carry out can be an opportunity for creative growth in your marriage.

Here's an unusual example. Randy and Marilyn had been married three years. Both were twenty-four. Exhibiting a great deal of maturity, they selected twelve couples for shared evenings in their home. Once a month they invited a couple for dinner. After dinner, they explained their idea of learning about marriage from others and asked their friends to talk about the strengths of marriage from their experience. Since Randy and Marilyn did not have children, they particularly wanted to know what effect the birth of children had on the relationship of the couple. Of the twelve couples, three had been married over twenty years, six couples were married between ten and twenty years, and three couples under ten years.

At my last meeting with them, they shared their decision not to have children—at least right now. Randy and Marilyn gained many insights from this experience. I would guess they also provided the stimulus for twelve couples to do some rethinking of their relationships.

Any really useful tool for self-help has four important characteristics. First, the project represents a joint commitment of time to and for each other. The second characteristic is that the couple shares the experience and their reactions and reflections with each other. The third factor is the change of pace provided for the couple. Any self-help project can get you "out of the routine." Regular patterns of activity are changed. Finally, the experience provides new data or variety which is stimulating to the couple.

Here are some examples of actual experiences couples shared with me in their own efforts:

"We are joining a restaurant dinner club to visit different places to eat out at least once a month."

"Joyce and I are becoming members of a church to establish a new relationship between us, our religious beliefs, and other persons who share those beliefs."

"We are establishing a new part-time business adventure. We share equally in the investment in the marriage and in our new project."

"Bill and I are designing and building a new home. We've always wanted to do this. We feel closer together in this project than we have in a long time."

"We are together selecting and purchasing a new wardrobe for both of us. [Probably nothing aids one's ego more than feeling that he is admired by the person to whom he is married.—Author.] After our joint diet effort, this is our reward to each other."

"John and I are writing two articles together and seeking to have them published. I'm really excited about this."

"For a month we are exchanging gifts or energies, creative efforts, or specific requests on a regular schedule. One day a week each of us is 'slave' to the other partner. We can ask for any favor we want. It's a game, but it has been a lot of fun so far."

Many other ideas can be utilized as ways of freshening, invigorating, or stimulating your marriage relationships. Why don't the two of you put the book down and make a list now?

13.

Special Problems in Marriage

THIS CHAPTER INCLUDES a potpourri of issues raised in some marriages which may not be present in the majority. These problems occur with some frequency in counseling.

Depression

Depression may be the number one mental health symptom in the world. That pervasive discontent and dejected feeling, often called the "blues," can adversely affect the marriage.

Depression is the most frequently used word to describe emotional symptoms. Most of us are depressed at some time in our lives. Some do not recognize the symptoms. They drag through each day, not knowing that life can be different. What they experience as "normal" may be depression.

To be depressed is to function at a low level of emotional interaction—to be blocked from within oneself. Since this is a complex phenomenon, it may appear in different symptoms, with passive, defensive, aggressive, or other overtones. At the simplest level, depression is the experience of life as "down." When I feel drained of energy, apathetic, and just "can't get excited about anything," I am probably depressed.

Five Contributing Causes

Five basic causes of depression have clearly emerged in the people I've known in professional counseling. The factors contributing to depression are:
1. Chemical or biological imbalance
2. Unresolved guilt
3. Unexpressed anger
4. Fear of failure
5. A sense of isolation.
Let's examine them more closely.

Chemical or Biological Imbalance

In my experience, less than 10 percent of the cases of depression I encounter are of a physical origin. What is called "post partum depression," the letdown experience in the first few months after the birth of a child, is common among younger females. A few cases related to levels of blood sugar or dietary imbalance are also seen. The great majority of those I have referred to medical doctors for a checkup receive negative reports. Yet most cases of depression are treated by chemotherapy, or medication. A good physician will acknowledge that this is only a stopgap treatment of the symptoms, while ignoring the cause. My own clinical knowledge says that you cannot touch the emotional cause of depression with a chemical solution. Let's look further, then, at the kinds of nonchemical "downs" we experience.

Unresolved Guilt

Guilt takes a heavy toll on emotional energy. Hobart Mowrer suggested in his writings that "confession to others is an appropriate way of treating depression." [1] This is based on his observation that a good deal of depression is caused by guilt. Relieving my guilt frees my emotional resources for other uses. A good place to uncover the cause of your "down" feelings is to examine your relationships. Have I wronged someone? Can I identify a relationship about which I feel guilty? Admitting those feelings resolves much of the depression.

Rational, or real guilt, is different from irrational, or neurotic, guilt. The real thing, known as rational guilt, can be dealt with through action. I can make restitution in some form—an apology, a repayment, or a substitutionary action. Verbal offenses can be made right verbally; physical offenses, with physical actions. There is a balancing action for the cause of my guilt.

On the other hand, neurotic or irrational guilt is usually unknown to anyone but me. I alone must deal with my guilt. Much of this neurosis is based on my inability to live up to the expectations I assume others have of me. Some of my guilt may result from my own unrealistic demands on myself. When I recognize that I cannot be perfect, I begin to resolve this guilt. It is this neurotic feeling that is best addressed in Fritz Perls's now-famous lines:

I do my thing and you do your thing.
I am not in this world to live up to your expectations,

---

[1] Hobart Mowrer, *The Crisis in Psychiatry and Religion* (New York: Van Nostrand, 1961); and *The New Group Therapy* (New York: Van Nostrand Reinhold Co., 1964).

And you're not in this world to live up to mine.
You are you and I am I,
And if by chance we find each other,
It's beautiful.

Unexpressed Anger

Anger hidden within us is another major cause of depression. These feelings may create some physical symptoms such as an ulcerated stomach or intestinal disturbances. People plagued with guilt frequently suffer headaches and neck pains. These unexpressed feelings do damage to us—not only internally, but they also can create destructiveness in our relationships. Hidden anger has a way of erupting when we least expect it to and often at a most inopportune moment.

How often our anger toward a spouse is vented on a child! It may be the angry frustration of the job that has depressed us but our family members who are hurt by its release. Hurt and anger are opposite poles of a continuum. At one end is anger and at the other end is hurt. Often when I feel hurt, I get angry and retaliate. Sometimes when I'm angry and do not express it, I get hurt and weak. I need to express both feelings. Unexpressed anger is like a sponge; it absorbs my energy and I begin to feel depressed.

Fear of Failure

When I feel as if I am going to fail, I sometimes react with passivity. This "trapped" or situational depression is frequent among males.

A forty-six-year-old man came for counseling on referral from his physician. He was depressed and had begun to lose his sexual drive. As we talked about his symptoms, I discovered that he was the vice-president of a family owned business. While he made a good salary, he was only two years younger than the president of that firm. He had peaked out vocationally, but he was unable to express his feeling of being trapped. He needed the security of his present salary, but he felt no challenge for the future. He was depressed bcause he saw nineteen years of boredom ahead of him.

The same kind of feelings are present when a couple feels locked into a marriage that is "going nowhere." Teenagers experience this depression when they feel that their family members are just putting up with each other because "they have to do it." When I face a situation in which I feel trapped or a problem I can't overcome, a profound sense of heaviness drags me "down." I am depressed.

A Sense of Isolation

The fifth contributor to depression is a feeling of being alone. "Feeling cut off" is a description I hear often.

A sixty-two-year-old woman was depressed. Her husband had died five years earlier; and since he was gone, she had become less and less active. She spent a week or more at a time in her apartment seeing no one but her cat. She was isolated! Her depression had a real cause. She began to feel better simply because she got dressed up and came to my office. She had no serious mental problem, but her "homework" became the therapy of active involvement. As she reentered her world and engaged people in relationships, her "down" feelings vanished.

Feeling isolated within yourself—that sense of being "lonely in a crowd"—is dealt with much like the widow in her world. Break out of your shell and make contact with another person.

The central issue in marriage is the couple's handling of

depression. The nondepressed partner who blames himself will increase the impact of this episode on the total relationship.

Nathan became depressed when his father, who was just fifty-five, suddenly died. After several months Dinah began to feel that something was wrong with their marriage. Nathan's quiet brooding seemed to be an indication that she had failed him.

When Nathan got into treatment, Dinah was reassured about her contribution to his temporary mental and emotional setback. Concentrating less on her imagined weakness, she had more energy to be supportive toward Nathan. As he brought his fear of death into focus and released his hidden grief over the loss of his father, Nathan's spirits lifted. Dinah did some maturing too, and their marriage was back to a level of satisfactory responsiveness.

Vocational Stress

Insufficient research has been published to measure the impact of vocational stress on marriage. Experiences with couples indicate a strong relationship between job satisfaction and marital fulfillment.

Dale was worried about his job. The company he worked for had been sold to a larger organization. Every employee was under reevaluation and assessment as the two companies merged. He talked to Lillian about his hopes and fears at times, but he felt she was preoccupied with the children. What he heard from her was a resistance to a possible move. She spoke of her fears of leaving friends and the only home she had ever known if he was transferred to a new city.

When Dale talked to me, he spoke very critically of Lillian. "She just doesn't care what I am going through," he concluded. A long series of negative and suspicious comments about his wife had preceded his summation. "I'll probably just move out and try life alone for awhile; I don't know what else to do."

I saw the picture from a different perspective. Dale felt watched and under judgment during this merger. Since he was only a salaried employee, he had no input in the decision to sell the company. He was angry that he might lose the position that he had developed over the twelve years he had been there. He tried not to express his anger—or even to acknowledge it—at work. When I asked how long he had felt discouraged about his marriage, the beginning of the problem coincided with the announcement of the company's sale.

With time, Dale could see how his frustration with the job had been converted into criticism of Lillian. He could not control his vocational fate. As a result he turned his attention to their marriage—critical.

A real crisis occurred for them when Dale was offered a promotion with another firm. He decided to take the job. Lillian expressed her fears and ties to their home. By this time Dale understood what had happened to him, and his patient understanding while she worked through her feelings brought them closer together.

Remembering the intensity of Dale's anger, I knew that his and Lillian's relationship might have been lost at two points. The first was when Dale felt trapped and dependent about his job. His attacks on Lillian were attempts to gain control of something in his life. When this insight registered, some security was restored. Fortunately, his experience was useful in the second point of tension. Dale could appreciate Lillian's frustration at being forced to leave home. As they confronted each other, she saw how unsupportive she had been earlier. They were drawn closer to each other because of the way they handled these stresses.

Moving ranks next to building a home as a major stress factor in a marriage. This couple, and their children, had

much work to do as they adjusted. The new stress was more
visibly external; they were all moving together and needed
each other during this transition.

The hidden stress of the earlier period was more subtle.
Dale had tried to deal with it alone. When his attempts at
communication failed, he was convinced that no one else
cared. His marriage too seemed in jeopardy. He summed up
the significant meaning of their transition in our last session:
"If I had not come to see what was happening to me, I
would be moving to another state, alone and divorced. I
know we have work to do in our relationship, but I feel very
hopeful we can do it together."

Vocational stress handled independently can produce un-
expected results in the relationship which are not always
positive. When it is acknowledged and faced within the
structure of the marital union, the chances of destruction
are minimized.

It is most difficult for any of us to face the things we cannot control in our lives. Since vocations often fall into this
arena, we tend to let our occupational choices and stresses
become buried in what appears to be more easily controlled
experience. Numerous couples have been divorced because
they failed to recognize the vocational stress that contributed
to marital disharmony.

14.

Make Your Marriage Dreams Come True!

As a public speaker one of my most frequent themes is marriage. In this concluding chapter I want to share with you some ideas that have been part of my most popular presentation, "Make Your Marriage Dreams Come True!"

My office at times seems like a receptacle for broken dreams. Couples who have been derailed and discouraged often seek marital counseling. Others are divorced and discontent with their efforts at fulfilling their marital dreams. Some feel crushed by the weight of their personal sense of failure. The "man in my dreams" (or woman) may not become a reality; you can be married under orange blossoms and get a lemon just the same. Love is sometimes blind, but marriage is always a real eye opener! Marriage dreams need action and growth to be fulfilled.

There are three things that every marriage needs to make our dreams come true. *They are these: every marriage needs a gift, every marriage needs a goal, and every marriage needs a God.*

A Gift

Every marriage needs a gift. Little things do mean a lot, to men as well as women. Men are just as sensitive to the forgotten occasion as women are. When we forget each other, the feeling develops in our marriage that we have been taken for granted. It is a difficult feeling to change, but some people do decide to work at it. I am reminded of the man who had an argument with his wife early one morning. She had really roasted him before he left for work. He felt blue all day—hurt, depressed, and "down." So he stopped by to see his minister on his way home from the office. "My wife and I have been having a real tough time, and we had a fight this morning to end all fights," he said. "I don't even know whether she'll let me in the door when I get home." The minister said, "Tell me about what is going on with the two of you. Have you told your wife lately that you love her?" The man said, "Well, we have been married fifteen years. I told her that on our wedding night, isn't that enough?" The minister said, "No, no; it needs to be heard more often. Let me suggest this. On the way home, buy a box of candy and a bouquet of flowers. Go in and give her the gifts, put your arms around her, give her a big kiss, and tell her that you love her. I think things will be a lot better."

So the man bought the candy and flowers on his way home that night. When he opened the front door, his wife wasn't around. He said in a loud voice, "Hello, I'm home." Hearing some noise in the kitchen, he went back and found her standing over the hot stove, perspiring, with her hair sticking to the back of her neck. He went up to her, put his arms around her, kissed her on the back of the neck and said, "Darling, I love you." She turned around, and he pushed the bouquet of flowers into her arms along with the box of candy. But she burst into tears. He hadn't expected that; after all the minister had said it would work. But he paused for a moment, and she finally said, "This has been a terrible day. This morning the washing machine broke down and the basement is flooded. This afternoon Johnny broke his arm and I had to spend the afternoon at the hospital. And now you come home drunk."

Sometimes the gifts that we need come so infrequently that they almost seem like drunkenness. If a gift seems out of character, too much time has passed between the experience of giving. Real giving develops slowly but surely. We remember the little things. Relationships happen in the living room and the kitchen which prepare us for what we share in the bedroom. Love is not just sex and sexual giving; it is the giving of ourselves to each other. Husbands and wives are like fires; when they are unattended, they go out.

The most important gifts of life are not material. They are not candy and flowers or rings and trinkets. The best gifts are parts of ourselves—the gifts of personhood. May I give you a short course in human relations? Married and single people can use these guides to get along with each other.

The five most important words that you can ever learn are these: I am proud of you. The four most important words are: What do you think? The three most important words are: I am sorry. The two most important words are: Forgive me. The single most important word in relationship is: We. The gift of caring and remembering are most important. Best of all is the gift of self. A successful marriage is really a 60–40 proposition, with both partners being responsible for the 60 percent. If you are good at math, you will see that adds up to 120 percent for a bonus situation. If both partners are only responsible for 40 percent, what you get is less than 100 percent. If your marriage is winding up a little bit short, or other relationships are dissatisfactory, ask yourself how far you are going in sharing? How much of yourself are you really giving?

What you are is far more important than what you have.
I work with teenagers as well as husbands and wives. One
common phrase I hear from them regularly is, "My parents
give me everything but themselves." What young people
want from their parents is not things; they want the gift of
self—personal time and energy invested in them. That is
also what wives and husbands want from each other. The
basic questions in life are really answered in terms of relationships.

Someone has said that life's essentials are summed up in
these three questions: Who am I? What am I here? Where
am I going? All of those questions are answered in relationships. We discover who we are in response to others. Why we
are here is known in interaction with others. Our purpose
and meaning in life is revealed in relationship to people.
That is especially true of the most intimate of relationships
—marriage. Every marriage needs a gift, the gift of what we
are given fully to each other. It will help marriage dreams
come true.

A Goal

Every couple needs a goal. Marriage is not two people
standing eye to eye staring at each other. It is two standing
shoulder to shoulder looking ahead at the same goal, an-
ticipating with each other. Sometimes people get married
and they create competition. They sing to each other that
little song which says, "Anything you can do I can do better." Competition in a marriage brings hatred and contempt.
In an apocryphal story, two Irishmen named Kelly and
Murphy were in constant competition with each other. They
argued over everything. God finally got so tired of their
arguing that he sent an angel down to put an end to it. The
angel got Kelly to the side and said, "Kelly, I want you and

Murphy to quit your fighting with each other. I'll give you anything you want as long as you'll let Murphy have two of them." Kelly thought for a minute and he said, "Let me understand this. If I get one brass band leading me down the street when we have a parade, Murphy gets two?" The angel said, "Right." "If I get one gold Cadillac, Murphy gets two?" Kelly said. "That's right," said the angel. "Now hurry up, Kelly. What is your wish?" Kelly thought for a moment longer and, born out of the competition that breeds hatred, he said, "I wish for one glass eye!"

When people begin to compete with each other in marriage that is exactly what happens. We destroy each other. We take away the joy of living. We ruin each other. We steal the love, we destroy the trust, we lose respect, and we fail at sharing with each other. The goal of marriage is to take away loneliness. The Genesis account says that everything God made in the world was good except for the fact that the man he had made was lonely. God created a woman to keep man from being lonely. I saw a poster which eloquently says, "No man can live with the terrible knowledge that he is not needed." Basic to everyone is the need to have someone share life with him. Anyone who says he doesn't need anybody is fooling himself; he has missed one of the central facts of life. Every marriage needs sharing.

The rabbis recognized it when they wrote about the creation of women. It is written that she was not made from man's head to rule over him. She was not made from man's feet to be trampled by him. She was taken from a rib of his side to be equal with him, from under his arm to be protected by him, from near his heart to be loved by him. It is so easy for us to lose sight of the goal to love and fulfill each other. That is what life is about! Loving each other is far more important than anything that goes on in a sanctuary. God made the home before he made the church. If you love each other, what happens everywhere else is improved. If you don't love each other, no rituals can substitute for your sharing.

The absence of a shared goal creates emptiness and a void that nothing else in your life can fill. It is too easy for us to build individual worlds apart from each other, isn't it?

Some of you are golfing widows. Some men build their individual worlds in pursuit of a little ball. I remember the story of the fellow who so pursued the golf ball that his wife gave up on him. She said, "I am tired of playing second fiddle to a golf bag. Either you get home today at noon and take the family on a picnic or our marriage is over. I will call a locksmith and change the door, and I am going to put everything you own out in the street.

Of course, he didn't take her seriously. Most of us don't take threats seriously because we are part of the pattern. We have a system that works. Alcoholics have partners in the marriage who carry on their half of the bargain. He nags so that she can drink, and she drinks so that he can nag. We balance the relationship with each other. If something is consistently happening in your marriage, you can be sure that both of you are balancing the act. You need a catcher for every pitcher. This lady had tolerated her husband's behavior and he didn't take her seriously. He went to the golf course. It got dark, and he finally came home. But this time she was serious. Everything he owned was packed on the front porch. He tried his lock and his key wouldn't work. He finally rang the bell, and she came to the door. He said, "Let me explain; this has been a terrible day. We started early, and on our way to the golf course I ran out of gas. I had to walk a mile to get some gas. Then we had a flat tire, and the spare was flat. We had to roll the tire a mile and a half back to the gas station. We finally got to the course and had a great first tee. On the second tee Fred had a heart attack. I ran back to the club house to get some help, and nobody was there. I ran back to Fred, and found he had died. Honey, that is the way it was all day: hit the ball, drag Fred; hit the ball, drag Fred!"

When we start building individual worlds that separate us, everything else gets out of whack. We begin to lose real values and basic perception about life. Everything else loses its value too; life becomes like "hitting the ball and dragging Mary." The marriage partner is dead weight! It is important to discover where our values are. Marriage dreams come true when we share with each other a goal. A goal that is meaningful, personal, and unique is a real marital plus!

A God

I believe that every marriage needs a God. I do not mean the God of ritual. Doing certain things is not enough to put God in your marriage. Worship is important, but we also have some problems when we worship together. Especially when we have our children in worship it can get a little bit frustrating. Little Johnny came to church with his parents. The preacher talked endlessly. Mother was doing everything she could to keep Johnny interested. She looked on the side of the church and she said, "Johnny, do you know what that flag is?" He whispered, "The American flag." She had him count the colors and the stripes and the stars until he became bored again. Then she said, "Johnny, do you know what the other flag is?" He said, "That is the Christian flag." She had him count the colors and go through the process again. In that particular church they had a gold flag with the names embroidered on it of the men who died in the military. She finally said, "Johnny, do you know what kind of flag that is?" He said, "No, I don't." She said, "That is the flag for all the boys who died in the service." Dryly Johnny looked at her and said, "Which one, Mother, morning or evening?"

Sometimes trying to worship as a family is only ritual.

What I am talking about is that every marriage needs a relationship with our personal God. The family who prays—really prays—stays together. In a meaningful way God changes the relationship. The closer we get to God the closer we get to each other.

Some years ago we were on vacation in California. At Shasta Lake we were watching some water activities. I watched two people ski behind a boat in the middle of the vast lake. When the skiers set their legs toward each other and held tightly to the rope, they could push their bodies almost at a forty-five degree angle. When they worked at it, even in the water, they could get further and further apart. But if they relaxed at all, the force of the boat skimming through the water brought the skiers back next to each other until they could touch hands. That close they could speak even with the noise of the boat and the sounds of the water around them. That is the way God is in our lives. If we resist each other we can push ourselves out just as far as we wish, but the minute we relax the force of God draws us closer to each other. The closer you get to God, the closer the two of you are going to be to each other. The closer your family gets to God the closer you are going to be to each other. That is what having a God does to make marriage dreams come true.

Louis Mayer, the famous motion picture producer, tells this story about his boyhood. One day he got mad at his mother; he slammed the door as he left the house and said "Damn you!" The next day his mother packed a picnic lunch, and they went to one of the mountains near their home. After lunch with each other his mother said to him, "Louis, I want you to go to the edge of the cliff and yell 'Damn you' at the top of your lungs." He said, "I don't want to do that." She said, "Do it!" With that firmness in her voice, he went over and said faintly, "Damn you." She said, "That is not loud enough. Say it again." Finally, he got his

courage up and he screamed, "Damn you!" And he heard
the echo: "Damn you; (more faintly) damn you; (very
faintly) damn you." His mother said, "Now, Louie, I want
you to say, 'Bless you.'" That wasn't hard; he raised his voice
and said, "Bless you." And he heard the echo again: "Bless
you; (less loudly) bless you; (faintly) bless you." His
mother said, "Louie, if you go through life yelling 'Damn
you' at people, what you will hear is, 'Damn you, Louie,
damn you.' If you say, 'Bless you,' then what you will hear
is, 'Bless you, Louie, bless you.'" Marriage is like that too.
You don't make your marriage dreams come true by yelling
"Damn you." You do it by saying "Bless you." The presence
of God in our lives helps us say "Bless you" to each other.

Louis Evans's "A Prayer for a Bride and Groom" says it
well:

> O God of love, Thou hast established marriage for the
> welfare and happiness of mankind. Thine was the plan, and
> only with Thee can we work it out with joy. Thou hast said,
> "It is not good for man to be alone; I will make a helpmate
> for him." Now our joys are doubled, since the happiness of
> one is the happiness of the other. Our burdens now are halved,
> since when we share them, we divide the load. Bless this
> husband, bless him as the provider of nourishment and rai-
> ment, and sustain him in all the exactions and pressures of
> his battle for bread. May his strength be her protection, his
> character be her boast and her pride, and may he so live that
> she will find in him the haven for which the heart of woman
> truly longs. Bless this loving wife. Give her a tenderness that
> will make her great, a deep sense of understanding and a great
> faith in Thee. Give her that inner beauty of soul that never
> fades, that eternal youth that is found in holding fast the
> things that never age. Teach them that marriage is not merely
> living for each other; it is two uniting and joining hands to
> serve Thee. Give them a great spiritual purpose in life. May
> they seek first the kingdom of God in his righteousness and
> the other things shall be added unto them. May they not ex-

pect that perfection of each other that belongs alone to Thee. May they minimize each other's weaknesses, be swift to praise and magnify each other's points of comeliness and strength, and see each other through a lover's kind eyes. Now make such assignments to them on the scroll of Thy will as will bless them and develop their characters as they walk together. Give them enough tears to keep them tender, enough hurt to keep them humane, enough of failure to keep their hands clenched tightly in Thine, and enough success to make them sure they walk with God. May they never take each other's love for granted, but always experience that breathless wonder that exclaims, "Out of all this world, you have chosen me!" When life is done and the sun is setting, may they be found then as now, hand in hand, still thanking God for each other. May they serve Thee happily, faithfully together, until at last one shall lay the other into the arms of God. This we ask through Jesus Christ, great lover of our souls. Amen. [1]

These three ingredients assure couples the fulfillment of their marital dreams—sharing gifts, goals, and God.

Try marriage this way; you can avoid trying divorce.

---

[1] From the LP *Love, Marriage, and God,* by Louis Evans (Waco, Texas: Word Records, 1960) .